THE
SCHLEMIEL
AS
MODERN
HERO

THE UNIVERSITY OF CHICAGO PRESS / CHICAGO & LONDON

THE SCHLEMIEL AS MODERN HERO

Ruth R. Wisse

International Standard Book Number: 0–226–90311–7
Library of Congress Catalog Card Number: 72–160841
THE UNIVERSITY OF CHICAGO PRESS, CHICAGO 60637
THE UNIVERSITY OF CHICAGO PRESS, LTD., LONDON
© 1971 by The University of Chicago
All rights reserved. Published 1971
Printed in the United States of America

CONTENTS

ACKNOWLEDGMENTS

This work was originally a doctoral dissertation entitled, *The Schlemihl as Hero in Yiddish and American Fiction.* I am deeply grateful to my advisor, Louis Dudek, of the English Department at McGill University; to its chairman, Donald F. Theall; and to the founding chairman of the Jewish Studies Programme, Harry M. Bracken, for helping and encouraging me; and to Merrily Paskal, for being at McGill when I was.

Without the shared interest of my friends and family the book would have been a more dreary undertaking. Without the welcome intervention of Charlotte Mayerson it would not have been published.

A fellowship from the Canada Council provided financial and moral backing. The YIVO Institute for Jewish Research, in the person of its librarian, Dina Abramowicz, promptly filled all requests for material and information. My colleagues, Raymond Scheindlin and Gerald Blidstein, have generously and patiently helped me with explanations of terms and sources.

I am indebted to Irving Howe for his careful critical reading of the manuscript; to Rabbi David Hartman, whose thinking—even when not directly acknowledgeable—has so influenced the lives of his students; to Gita Rotenberg for good editorial advice.

I thank my husband for everything, in particular for listening to many dozens of jokes, not all of them funny.

My first advisors on this subject were Uriel Weinreich, then chairman of the Department of Linguistics at Columbia University, and later Max Weinreich, my most beloved teacher. They were the most exacting of teachers and also the kindest. This book, though unworthy of their standards, I dedicate to their memory.

INTRODUCTION

The capacity of East European Jewry of the past four centuries to maintain a disciplined and imaginative personal and communal life despite vicious, unrelenting harassment has not yet been adequately assessed by either the natural heirs or by students of comparative civilization. Among the former, the sentimentalists see the past in a frieze of silver-grey, the kneaded challahs forever on the Sabbath table and the slops conveniently banished. The strongarm survivalists resent the death of the Jews so bitterly they cannot allow them even a historical existence. Reading death back into everything, they deny Yiddish Jews their creative achievements, and thereby avoid the pain of acknowledging that anything died. For still others, the foreknowledge of its tragic end poisons any healthy enjoyment of the culture. Like my son who would punctuate renditions of Little Red Riding Hood with nervous inquiries about the wolf, they are too anxious about the villainy to appreciate the tale.

Yet before the destruction there was a civilization of considerable resiliency whose continuing ability to experience frustration without yielding to desperation or defeatism may be reason enough for winning our interest, particularly at this time. Pain thresholds vary among peoples as among people; the threshold of East European Jews was exceedingly high, perhaps even excessively high if pain is to serve as a warning of mortal danger. The community learned to absorb severe shock without abandoning the image of man to which it had pledged itself, and without losing its love or desire for life. Inevitably, the techniques of self-containment and self-control produced some self-disgust as well, and a great deal of bitterness. Yiddish humor is cuttingly sharp; it contains more of harshness than merriment. But on balance these techniques did preserve sanity and health and a spectacular energy that can be observed, even in America, in transplanted form.

The schlemiel is a character of folklore and fiction whose life-style is the sum of these techniques. He stands in the age-old company of fools, embodying the most outstanding folly of *his* culture: its weakness. Touchstone was harmless and charming; the schlemiel is harmless and disliked. Feste is vulnerable but wily; the schlemiel is vulnerable and inept. The schlemiel is neither saintly nor pure, but only weak. The sleight of hand of his comedy is intended to persuade us that this weakness is strength. In much the same way, the technique of adaptation required of the Jew that he reinterpret his weakness as its opposite, for how else could a weakling survive? By telling this kind of story:

A Jew went to visit Krotoshin, a town larger than his own, where he was publicly humiliated by the local chief of police. When he returned home, his neighbor taunted him, saying, "I hear you got your face slapped in the streets of Krotoshin." The Jew shrugged, "Krotoshin. Some place."

The refusal to be defined by others is not merely a convenient pose that can be assumed by anyone wanting to turn the tables on his oppressor. The tight internal structure of the Jewish community and the intricate code of behavior by which each individual governed his daily life produced this strong sense of identity as one of its by-products. Interestingly, in modern Jewish literature when the individual moves within his own community, its stultifying and repressive tendencies are emphasized; once the Jew emerges from this community to confront the wider world, his background is translated into a source of individual worth, strength of identity, even personal freedom.

For many reasons, some odd, others natural, this unlikely hero, the schlemiel, became a recurrent figure in American culture during the relative calm of the 1950s. The ninety-seven-pound weakling of the old Charles Atlas advertisements, but with the bias of the sales pitch on his side, he made his way into the popular culture, and then into good fiction where his success was so great as almost to defeat his claim to failure. The proliferation of the schlemiel has not gone unnoticed. However, like so much else in America, he stands cut loose from his roots, and neither he nor his audience seems aware of his origins. In the hope that the sixth sense is a welcome accessory, and with the full certainty that his past is at least as entertaining as his presence, the following pages attempt to provide a brief history of the literary schlemiel: he was born in Krotoshin.

THE
SCHLEMIEL
AS
MODERN
HERO

1. ASPECTS OF THE CHARACTER

The Political Schlemiel

Sometime during World War I, a Jew lost his way along the Austro-Hungarian frontier. Wandering through the woods late at night, he was suddenly arrested by the challenge of a border-guard: "Halt, or I'll shoot!" The Jew blinked into the beam of the searchlight and said:

"What's the matter with you? Are you crazy? Can't you see that this is a human being?"

The studied pathos of this joke is characteristic of schlemiel literature. Outrageous and absurd as his innocence may be by the normal guidelines of political reality, the Jew is simply rational within the context of ideal humanism. He is a fool, seriously—maybe even fatally—out of step with the actual march of events. Yet the impulse of the joke, and of schlemiel literature in general, is to use this comical stance as a stage from which to challenge the political and philosophic status quo.

So too when an Austrian officer pauses during training drill to ask: "Katsenstein, why does a soldier give up his life for his country?" Private Katsenstein replies: "You're right, Sergeant, why does he?"

Or in the negative counterpart of the joke, when the sergeant asks, "Why shouldn't a soldier walk near barracks with a burning cigarette?" Private Feldheim asks, "You're right, sergeant, why shouldn't he?"[1]

These jokes and their many likenesses are about non-military rather than antimilitary types. The responses are not in the spirit of conscious rebellion, but the naïve, wholly spontaneous questions of a different culture. It goes without saying that the jokes, structured on a rhythmic counter-point between two cultures represented by the brusque com-mand or rhetorical challenge and the innocent query, are not as naïve as their subjects. But the subjects of the jokes are simpletons, provoking our recognition that in an insane world, the fool may be the only morally sane man.

The reader will recognize in this paradox one of the most familiar situations of literature since the fool led Lear to self-knowledge some thirty-six decades ago. The Jewish schlemiel is merely one version of the fool, "a man who falls below the average human standard, but whose defects have been transformed into a source of delight."[2] The schle-miel shares many of the fool's characteristics and is used in many of the stock situations. As the cited jokes indicate, however, the schlemiel is also used as the symbol of an entire people in its encounter with surrounding cultures and its opposition to their opposition.

Though the Jewish fool began as a typical prankster and wit in the Middle Ages, his utility as a metaphor for Euro-pean Jewry was later perceived by the folk and its formal writers. Vulnerable, ineffectual in his efforts at self-advance-ment and self-preservation, he emerged as the archetypal

1. For similar jokes see Nathan Ausubel, ed., *A Treasury of Jewish Humor* (New York, 1951); Immanuel Olsvanger, ed., *Royte pomer-antsen* (New York, 1947); Salcia Landmann, *Jüdische Witze* (Munich, 1962); and subsequent references.

2. Enid Welsford, *The Fool, His Social and Literary History* (Glou-cester, Mass., 1966), p. xi.

Jew, especially in his capacity of potential victim. Since Jewry's attitudes toward its own frailty were complex and contradictory, the schlemiel was sometimes berated for his foolish weakness, and elsewhere exalted for his hard inner strength. For the reformers who sought ways of strengthening and improving Jewish life and laws, the schlemiel embodied those negative qualities of weakness that had to be ridiculed to be overcome. Conversely, to the degree that Jews looked upon their disabilities as external afflictions, sustained through no fault of their own, they used the schlemiel as the model of endurance, his innocence a shield against corruption, his absolute defenselessness the only guaranteed defense against the brutalizing potential of might. The most interesting schlemiels of folklore and literature are those in whom both attitudes find simultaneous expression, reflecting a genuine, sustained ambivalence on the part of the author and raconteur.

The generations of Jews who lived as God's people, sanctifying every act of private and communal life in accordance with their understanding of His Commandments, considered all afflictions as rebukes in His ongoing efforts to forge a righteous nation. The Jews of secular modern times, who saw themselves not only through God's judgment, but through the eyes of their neighbors, found their infirmity more difficult to interpret. There was now God's view, *and* Voltaire's. In fashioning the schlemiel, the Jew admits how weak and foolish he appears to those who dominate him, and up to a point, he shares their view: "The Jew is always better off than the apostate; the Jew can still convert, the apostate can't." Yet beyond that point, he does not submit to self-hatred, and stands proudly on his record. After all, so goes the inevitable dialectic, he survives. And after all, is he as foolish as he seems? And above all, who are *they*

to judge him? At its best, the finished irony holds both the
contempt of the strong for the weak and the contempt of
the weak for the strong, with the latter winning the upper
hand. The schlemiel is the Jew as he is defined by the anti-
Semite, but reinterpreted by God's appointee:

The Battle of Tannenberg was at its height when a czarist officer drew up his company and addressed them. "The
moment has come! We're going to charge the enemy. It'll
be man against man in hand to hand combat." In the company was a Jewish soldier who was not fond of the czar
or his war.

"Please sir, show me my man!" he cried, "Perhaps I can
come to an understanding with him."

The Historical Irony

The most highly sanctioned revelries in Jewish culture are
associated with the holiday of Purim when the rabbis pre-
scribe that a man must drink till he can no longer distinguish "cursed Haman" from "blessed Mordecai." The occasion for this intemperance is the defeat of Haman, the
most notorious anti-Semite before Hitler, at the hands of
Mordecai, an almost unique example of successful Jewish
statesmanship. Since this advanced degree of drinking in
an otherwise fairly sober culture seemed to require some
explanation, many interpretations of the passage were suggested, including the following: the rabbis wanted Purim
to take man momentarily beyond good and evil, into the
Messianic ideal world where there were no villains or heroes, and no need for alert moral awareness. The categories
of Haman and Mordecai were to be not inverted, but tran-
scended, as they would be in the golden age to come. It
seems, however, that the actual celebrations of Purim took

a less exalted form, drawing their models from the local festival practices. Purim pantomimes, known even in Talmudic times, were followed by masquerades of the Middle Ages, and later by Purim plays of Central and Eastern Europe. The Purim fool was a stock character.

In Purim plays dating from the end of the fifteenth century the comic figures were replicas of the German narr, as their very names—Hans Wurst, Pickelherring—reveal. Their characteristic mode was cynicism, and they were permitted crude jokes and slapstick burlesque.[3] In Eastern Europe, when the Jews lived in homogeneous enclaves steeped in their own cultural sources and bounded by their own institutions, Purim joking became more intellectually pointed, more dependent on Talmudic and rabbinic allusions. The Purim rabbi was a popular character, providing the opportunity for satire of casuistry and local communal abuses. In the nineteenth century, the Purim fool was used by reformers as a mouthpiece for social and personal satire.

The festival of Purim commemorates the decisive defeat of Haman in a political context intimately familiar to Jews of medieval and modern Europe. The Jews of Shushan, a sizable but unprotected minority, must depend on a felicitous combination of beauty, brains, and sheer good fortune to save them from annihilation. Modern Jewries could not fail to notice the sad contrast between Mordecai's successful statesmanship as recorded in the *Book of Esther* and the more limited effects of *shtadlones*—intervention with the authorities—in their own communities. So the role of Mordecai was gradually brought into line with actual ex-

3. Max Erik, *Di geshikhte fun der yidisher literatur fun di eltste tsaytn biz der Haskole tkufe* [The history of Yiddish literature from the earliest period to the Haskalah] (Warsaw, 1928), p. 147.

perience and he was played as a comic character, a hunch-backed *schlepper* who succeeds in spite of his bumbling rather than on account of his brilliance.

In a modern literary Purim shpil, based in part on folk motifs and traditional jesting practices, the poet Itsik Manger uses mock-Biblical form to emphasize the gulf between the victorious Purim story and contemporary ignominy. The classical figure of Mordecai in Manger's *Megile lider*[4] is superceded by a genuine schlemiel who is added to the narrative in order to reinforce the sense of contrast between Shushan and shtetl. Manger says in the preface: "The official Megila chroniclers failed to mention as important a personage as the tailor-apprentice Fastri-gossa, though his thwarted love for Queen Esther and his attack on King Ahasuerus were decisive in determining the course of events. . . . It seems that they didn't want to besmirch the Persian court legend with such ordinary mortals."

Fastrigossa is a poor young tailor who is in love with Esther before her candidacy for queen. When her uncle Mordecai decides that she should be offered up to King Ahasuerus as a live-in lobby for the Jewish cause, Fastri-gossa tries to lure her away to Vienna, and then, with equal lack of success, to assassinate the king. He is imprisoned, the "Zhids" are blamed for stirring up trouble, and before the action takes a turn for the better, he is hanged. The Purim shpil as a whole was, of course, committed to the tra-ditional happy ending, and we are allowed the final hanging of Haman and political entrenchment of Esther-Mordecai. But the introduction of Fastrigossa as the focal character enabled Manger to interpret the Megila as an East Euro-

4. Itsik Manger, *Megile lider* [Megila songs] (Warsaw, 1936).

pean Jewish text. The play concludes with a dirge sung by Fastrigossa's mother on the first anniversary of her son's death in which she roundly curses "Esther the whore" for not attending the funeral or taking the trouble to inquire after her former lover during the months he was rotting in jail. The weeping mother's curse is also extended to wealthy Uncle Mordecai in a blanket condemnation of those who are concerned with the making of Jewish history but have little regard for the fate of everyday Jews.

The schlemiel, Fastrigossa, who was once presumably too insignificant for inclusion in the Biblical narrative, now epitomizes a national condition. Superimposing modern helplessness over former glory, the *Megile lider* telescopes Jewish history to reveal its internal ironies. There is comedy in the beggarly tailors who consider themselves the legatees of that former splendor. There is yet subtler comedy in the play's sly contention that the tailors have developed a kinder, more generous and humane ethic than the Bible ever knew. Like the Jew in the military jokes, Fastrigossa is a weakling whose political characteristics are innocence and impotence, and like the raconteurs of those jokes which challenged the automatic assumptions of authority, Manger sides with the East European Jews in questioning the Biblical emphasis on political success. The Yiddish Jews standing before the Solomons, Davids, and Mordecais of their own historical lineage were as mocking in their self-assessment as when they faced the czars, emperors, and Polish nobility. Telling the story of Shushan in the European diaspora could sound like a taunt, as when you call a bald man "curly," or the guy on the canvas, "champ." But the taunt could also be reversed. Who was Mordecai anyway but a sycophant and a sneak? Was Esther more than a pretty whore? The activities of the strong-willed Biblical heroes sometimes seemed less than properly "Jewish," and their humble descendents could be fairly harsh about the morality of their forebears.

The Fools of Folklore

Yiddish folk humor yielded up a limitless variety of fools, most of whom challenged not the political status quo or the prestige of the Biblical canon, but the heavy emphasis in the culture on learning, and the singular status of the scholar. The best-known fool stories are those of the fictional fools' town Chelm: Once, during the period of penitential prayers, the old shammes (sexton) of Chelm complained that he was too old and too weak to make the rounds of all the Jewish homes, banging on the shutters to wake the inhabitants for midnight services. The people of Chelm called an assembly, considered the problem from all points of view, and concluded that it would be best to assemble all the shutters, stack them by the shammes' house, and have him bang on all of them at the same time.

Stories of Chelm, showing up the folly of its inhabitants, usually follow a single pattern—when a problem must be solved, the Chelmites come up with a formula that is theoretically correct, but practically absurd. To capture the moon, the Chelmites throw a burlap bag over the top of a barrel filled with water, and are subsequently incredulous when they hear reports of the moon's appearance elsewhere. As the Chelmites try to push a mountain a little further away from their town, thieves steal the jackets they have dropped behind them. The Chelmites conclude that they have pushed far enough, since their jackets are no longer visible. A Chelmite at a bright street-corner looks for a coin he has lost. "Did you drop it here?" he is asked. "No, I dropped it back there in the dark, but it's easier to look for it here by the light." In the same way that the Hasidic movement protested against the arid intellectualism of Talmudic scholasticism, these Chelm jokes ridicule sophistry, or sterility of thought, which is dissociated from practical experience. Intellectualism is here turned on its head. "All the strains of a highly intellectualistic culture are relaxed in these tales of incredible foolishness and innocence," as Howe and Greenberg have suggested. In fact, the intellectualism of the culture is under attack *for* its alleged foolishness and innocence.[5]

A common comedy turn of Yiddish humor and Yiddish literature is the matchmaker's successful negotiation between two families, only to discover at the eleventh hour that he has paired off two brides, this being the classic example of theoretical success and practical failure.[6]

A more complex mode of humor can be found among the famous local wits, who reveal the folly of their betters even as their own foibles are exposed. There are Shmerl Snitkever and Yosl Marshelik (area of Old Constantine); Froim Graydinger (Poland); Motke Khabad and Shayke Fayfer (Lithuania); and the peripatetic Hershel Ostropolier (Ukraine) whose exploits have been recounted and invented for almost 200 years. These clever fools lived literally by their wits, fearlessly unmasking the hypocrisies of the rich who pretend to be righteous and the limited

5. Irving Howe and Eliezer Greenberg, eds., *A Treasury of Yiddish Stories* (New York, 1953), p. 610. The examples of Chelm stories are taken from J. Kh. Ravnitski, *Yidishe vitsn* [Yiddish jokes] (New York, 1950) 2: 100–112.

6. See, for example, Mendele Mocher Sforim's *Fishke der krumer* [Fishke the Lame] and Sholom Aleichem's *Menahem Mendl* in which such incidents are recounted at length.

who pretend to be learned. In certain stories they are philosophic fools, using witty interpretations to take the sting
out of their anxiety and pain:

Once a fire broke out in the house where Motke Khabad was
living. As the house went up in flames, the inhabitants all rushed
outside in a frenzy. Some brought pails of water, but Motke stood
there laughing. "What are you laughing at?" they asked him.
Motke replied: "I see my revenge on the cockroaches."[7]

One night some thieves crept into Hershel Ostropolier's house.
They searched and searched and found nothing. His wife shook
Hershel. "Wake up! There are thieves in the house." "Be still,"
answered Hershel. "If we're quiet, maybe they'll leave us something when they go."[8]

The fools here triumph by their reinterpretation of an
intolerable situation. Freud, discussing humor as the highest of defensive processes, says: "It scorns to withdraw the
ideational content bearing the distressing affect from conscious attention . . . and thus surmounts the automatism of
defense. It brings this about by finding a means of withdrawing the energy from the release of unpleasure that is
already in preparation and of transforming it, by discharge,
into pleasure."[9] Humorous displacement is apparent in
these jokes, where an inappropriate response transforms a
desperate moment into a pleasurable one.

The anti-intellectualism of the Chelm stories merges, in
formal schlemiel literature, with the antirationalism of
these philosophic fool tales. The reader is invited to enter-
tain the paradoxical notion that the absurd interpretation of

7. J. L. Kahan, ed., *Yidisher folklor* [Yiddish folklore] (Vilna, 1938),
p. 197.
8. Bibliography of Hershel Ostropolier in Ezra Leher, *Hersheli
Meostropoli*, in the periodical *Teyatron*, Tel Aviv, 1967–68.
9. Sigmund Freud, *Jokes and Their Relation to the Unconscious*, trans.
James Strachey (New York, 1960), p. 233.

experience may permit optimism, whereas a rational explanation will never lead beyond despair. The reaction against rationalism is, of course, one of the hallmarks of modern literature, and Keats sets the tone when he mourns that "philosophy will clip an Angel's wings." Later in the century, as in *Hard Times*, only the circus is able to rescue rational man from the utilitarian fallacy. It is the spirit of Mrs. Ramsay that hovers over twentieth-century fiction, while her poor level-headed husband never does push his way from Q to R. In Yiddish fiction, antirationalism is offered up in a more specific context, as the only adequate response to an irrational onslaught of events. The Spinoza of Market Street, attic philosopher of Isaac Bashevis Singer's masterful story by that name, reacts to the punishing chaos of wartime by "coming to his senses," to unreason, which is the only reasonable thing he can do. After a lifetime of Spinozistic control, Dr. Fishelson blossoms into a fool.

There were individual fools in the Yiddish folk repertoire, and typological fools among whom are the *nar, tam, yold, tipesh, bulvan, shoyte, peysi, shmendrik, kuni lemel, shmenge, lekish,* and *lekish ber,* to name but a limited assortment.[10] The schlemiel originally derived from a different category, the catalog of the luckless or the inept, like the *schlimazl,* the *goylem, lemekh,* general terms, or more specifically, the *nisrof* (who was burned out), the *yored* (who had lost his fortune), the *onverer* (who had gone into bankruptcy), the *farshpiler* (who had lost his money gambling), or the plain *loy yutslakh,* the literal good-for-nothing. As the foregoing fool stories suggest, the distinction

10. For the most complete selection of terms, see Nokhum Stutchkof, *Der oytser fun der Yidisher shprakh* [Yiddish thesaurus] (New York, 1950), entry 340.

among these categories is blurred; the fool was luckless, and the inept man was likely to be considered a fool. In a culture teeming with figures of this unhappy sort, schlemiel was at first only one of a vast number of almost synonymous types, each of which, nevertheless, represented a somewhat different shade of folly or loss.[11]

The American distinction between the schlemiel and the schlimazl, summarized in the rule of thumb that says the former spills the soup, the latter is the one into whose lap it falls, provides a helpful basis for definition. The schlemiel is the active disseminator of bad luck, and the schlimazl its passive victim. Or, more sharply defined, the schlimazl happens upon mischance, he has a penchant for lucklessness, but the unhappy circumstances remain outside him, and always suggest the slapstick quality of surprise. The schlemiel's misfortune is his character. It is not accidental, but essential. Whereas comedy involving the schlimazl tends to be situational, the schlemiel's comedy is existential, deriving from his very nature in its confrontation with reality.[12]

A Social Schlemiel

The first literary work to lend prestige to the term and character of the schlemiel was the novel by Adalbert von Chamisso, published in Germany in 1813.[13] Conceived as a fairy tale, *Peter Schlemihl* clearly reflected many of the

11. See Appendix.

12. There is some discussion of the derivation of the term and some attempt at definition in B. J. Bialostotski, *Yidisher humor un yidishe letsim* [Jewish humor and Jewish fools] (New York, 1963), pp. 35–36.

13. Adalbert von Chamisso, *Peter Schlemihl*, trans. Leopold von Lowenstein-Wertheim in *Three Great Classics* (New York, 1964), pp. 11–89. Chamisso heard the term schlemiel from Hitzig, who presumably had it from Heine. On the schlemiel in Heine's opus, see Hannah Arendt, "The Jew as Pariah," in Arthur A. Cohen's, *Arguments and*

author's personal anxieties, and the choice of this comic German-Jewish term for the hero's name was probably less a tribute to the children of the Jew, Hitzig, to whom the book was dedicated, than a comment on the "Jewish" insecurities of its decidedly Christian author. Chamisso was born a Frenchman, but his family was forced to flee the Revolution, and though he spent his youth and adolescence in Berlin, he could never feel himself to be a Prussian. As he wrote to his friend, Madame de Staël, "I am nowhere at home. I am a Frenchman in Germany and a German in France. A Catholic among Protestants, a Protestant among Catholics, a Jacobin among aristocrats, an aristocrat among democrats."

Peter, the persona-narrator, is a comic Faust who sells his shadow to a sinister man-in-grey in return for Fortunatus' lucky purse. While it is pleasant to have unlimited monies, a man cannot live in society without his shadow, and poor Mr. Schlemihl quickly discovers that he is consigned to loneliness, and the easy prey of blackmailers, until he can regain his useless but indispensable extension of himself.

A novelistic trifle when compared to the work in whose shadow it lies, *Peter Schlemihl* is effective within its self-imposed limits in evoking the anxieties of exclusion. The moral fable is neatly summarized by the narrator in his own conclusion:

Remember, my friend, while you live in the world to treasure first your shadow and then your money. But if you choose to live for your inner self alone, you will need no counsel of mine.[14]

Doctrines: A Reader of Jewish Thinking in the Aftermath of the Holocaust (New York-Philadelphia, 1970, pp. 24–49. Unfortunately I came upon this essay too late to involve its ideas in this chapter.

14. *Peter Schlemihl*, p. 89.

But this bit of homiletic advice does not do justice to the real theme of the work, namely, the consequences of an almost arbitrary removal from the bosom of society. The subject's fear of exposure to light, his frequent flights and attempted changes of identity, are all simple but accurate correlatives for the psychic condition of the marginal man.

The shadow is that extension of the self which is visible to others though extraneous to its owner. In the self-sufficiency of his room Peter does not miss his shadow, but the moment he attempts to mingle in society, he is mocked and ostracized. Chamisso's book, which broadened the meaning of the word schlemiel to include the outsider, comically and clumsily alienated from bourgeois conformity, treats this exclusion as a highly unfortunate condition, and one to be corrected. Peter learns a hierarchy of values: money, the lucky purse, is a completely external commodity, that ought not to be bartered away for your shadow. The image you project, still merely an extension of your essential self, is a good deal more important than possessions, but less important than "your inner self alone." Reputation is worth more than goods, but in the final analysis, the shadow is also expendable. Chamisso's work anticipates the theme of all schlemiel literature in which both possessions and reputation are freely sacrificed to protect the inner self alone.

A Hasidic Fool

The genesis of the literary schlemiel within the context of Yiddish literature is the tale of Rabbi Nachman of Bratzlav entitled "A Story about a Clever Man and a Simple Man" (A mayse mit a khokhm un a tam) (about 1805?).[15]

15. Nahman ben Simhah of Bratzlav, *Seyfer sipurey masyot* [Stories] (New York, 1951). Retold by Martin Buber, translated by Maurice

Rabbi Nachman, a great-grandson of Israel Baal Shem Tov, the founding figure of the Hasidic movement, was himself one of the great Hasidic teachers, who turned to storytelling in his later years as a more effective and more personal means of communicating with his student-followers than formal explication had been able to provide. Rabbi Nachman's recourse to the language of imagery rather than law was in the mystical tradition of the Cabalists, and his use of the Yiddish tale to dramatize his teachings had become a standard technique of Hasidic pedagogy even before his time. Compared to the anecdotal and homiletic style of the typical tales, however, his lengthy stories are unique in their complexity and in their simultaneous appeal to psychological realism, suspense, and even sensuous description. They were intended for those who could not look directly into the secrets of the Zohar but required a homier layer of allegory to introduce its mystery teachings. Their bias is obviously for intense feeling over and against intellectual stolidity. Rabbi Nachman attempted to capture the emotional, imaginative involvement of his students, their "soul's response" to his teachings, and not simply their intellectual assent. In both their form and thematic content, the stories exalt the instinctive response of devotion over even the highest achievement of mind.

This is particularly true of "The Clever Man and the Simple Man," the impact of which must be weighed against the previously unassailable prestige of the clever man in Jewish history since the dispersion. The study of Torah is one of the highest mitsvoth, or commandments, and the one most deeply respected by the culture at large. The Hasidic

---

Friedman in *The Tales of Rabbi Nachman* (Bloomington, Ind., 1962), pp. 71–94. Translations are from this edition, occasionally modified according to the original.

challenge to the authority of intellectualism is contained within this parabolic tale of Rabbi Nachman's, the bias of which is totally with the simple man, although the clever man is undoubtedly the more interesting figure by literary or psychological standards.

Two sons of two neighboring fathers are left orphaned. One is a clever son; the second is a simpleton. The clever son sells his father's house and goes out into the world where his rich intelligence wins him success at every kind of endeavor. He masters the skills of trade and finance, the art of sculpting, the craft of the goldsmith, the science of medicine, surpassing all others in each of these fields. But the same restless drive that propels him to master a succession of difficult skills, stirs up dissatisfaction and anxiety once those skills have been mastered. His aesthetic standards are so high that a perfectly tailored suit will displease him because of a minor irregularity in one of the cuffs. And since the aesthetic perfection of his own work is far beyond the appreciation of his audience, its very praise is more insult than compliment or balm.

In the meantime, the simpleton inhabits his father's house, lacking the imagination to do otherwise. He becomes a shoemaker, but Rabbi Nachman, who was far from projecting an ethic of satisfaction in labor, takes pains to tell us what a poor craftsman he was: his shoes were like triangles.

Poverty and lack of skill do not impair, however, the simple man's joy in living. When hungry, he munches on a crust of bread, exclaiming, "Wife, this is the tenderest piece of roast I have eaten in many a day." When thirsty, he drinks water, praising it as superior wine, most excellent mead. His shabby pelt is a fur coat in the winter, a silk caftan on the Sabbath. Undaunted by reality, the simple man lives happily, one day at a time.

Eventually, the two childhood friends are reunited, and the clever man, having no comfortable place to lodge, becomes a sojourner in the simple man's home. The parable becomes most explicit when the king of the country, hearing of these two dichotomous types, and curious to meet them, sends separate messengers for the two men. Upon receiving the invitation, the simple man goes whence he was summoned, and finding favor with everyone is rewarded by ever more prestigious offices until he is made first minister of the realm. The clever man challenges his messenger, asking whether he has ever actually seen the king whose invitation he carries, and when his doubts are confirmed, sets out to explode the myth of authority. Everywhere people serve the king without ever having seen him, and the clever man's skepticism regarding the ruler's actual existence grows unchecked. He suffers for his incredulity, because people do not take kindly to his challenges and denials; when he meets the simple man again, after a long interval, their roles have been reversed—the clever man is a lowly outcast while the simple man is one of the most admired persons in the land.

The clever man then inquires into the sources of the other's good fortune; the simple man replies that the king made him his minister, and conferred all his prestige upon him:

"What," said the clever man, "you too are gripped by this madness and believe in a King! I tell you there is no King."

"How can you suggest so monstrous a thing?" cried the minister. "I see the King's face daily."

"What makes you think," jeered the clever man, "that he with whom you speak is actually the King? Were you intimate with him from childhood on? Did you know his father and grandfather and can say that they were Kings? Men have told you that this is the King. They have fooled you."

This last confrontation is highly appropriate in terms of the story, since the reader has previously noted how easily the simple man creates the illusion he then calls reality. There is a real possibility that his faith in the king is a similar self-delusion. But at this juncture of the story, the simple man is the author's spokesman, and though he cannot prove the reality of his knowledge, he has the final say in the argument:

Then the minister said to him, "So do you still continue, then, to live in your subtleties and not see life? You asserted once that it would be easier for you to decline into my simplicity than for me to rise to your cleverness. But I now see that it is harder for you to attain my simplicity."

Although not the end of the tale, this is the moment at which the clever man is overcome, and his later admission of the king's existence is—as Buber in translating perceived —a decided anticlimax.

Rabbi Nachman's story is more involved in suggesting the psychological dangers of a speculative intelligence than in warning against the religious hazards of empirical enquiry. The clever man is so demanding that his very best efforts do not quite achieve his impossible ideals of perfection, and he is so concerned with rational proofs that he is finally incapable of responding to an existential summons. The clever man's intelligence, which becomes increasingly negative, or skeptical, as the story progresses, engenders doubt and dissatisfaction, until he becomes wholly incapable of any positive action or feeling.

The simple man, not limited by his intelligence, has never even sought to make a distinction between fact and illusion.

When the realities are insufficient, he turns to illusions, and when he receives an unanticipated call, he answers without questioning its legitimacy. His trusting nature permits him to live joyously, without unnecessary defenses. It is one of the simple man's great accomplishments, and one of the nicest touches of the story, that he responds to the frequent taunts of his neighbors with disarming gaiety: "Ay friend, just see how foolish I am! You can be a good deal cleverer than I and still be a proper fool." The story finds the simple man laudable not for his simplicity, but for its by-products, particularly the ability to live richly in the present with no care for "image" nor any need to protect his ego. The clever man is beset by growing insecurity, a fear of erring that is tantamount to a fear of living. Rabbi Nachman was deeply concerned with the dangers of European rationalism and empirical philosophy, and with the stultifying rigidity of Talmudic study as it had developed within the Torah community. His story, reversing the traditional values of the Talmudic culture, warns of what happens to the spirit of the man whose highest resource is his own mind, however great. The clever man seems to be able to achieve all excellence in his own person, but as soon as the immediate or cosmic environments thrust themselves upon him, he finds himself inadequate to meet their challenges. Despite its allegorical trappings, the story puts the clever and simple men to a basic pragmatic test, the criteria of which are worldly success, happiness, and healthy psychic survival. The simple man is not a natural saint; in fact his reliance on faith seems no more than a compensation for his lack of the power to reason. Nevertheless, and whatever its origins, his trust brings him the trust of others and enables him to take full advantage of any and all opportunities.

The distinction between rationalism and faith remained a

popular subject of Yiddish literature even after it was taken over by the secularists. The figure of the simple man continued to be used, as Rabbi Nachman here uses it, to demonstrate the real advantage of faith, than which nothing in the modern world seems more foolish, over reason and intelligence, the highest accomplishments of the unfettered mind. In the later secular works, faith is not a matter of religious credence, but the habit of trusting optimistically in the triumph of good over evil, right over wrong. It is also the dedication to living *as if* good will triumph over evil and right over wrong.

In Jewish experience of the nineteenth and twentieth centuries, such a belief was hard to sustain for anyone who troubled with empirical data. Yiddish writers—and the folk that created Yiddish folklore—recognized the foolishness, if they did not admit the absurdity, of such faith when every circumstance of daily life provided evidence against it. Indeed, many writers lashed out against the dumb trust in passivity, demanding in its stead a show of angry protest: Y. L. Peretz's famous story, "Bontshe Shvayg," now widely misread as a study of sainthood, is actually a socialist's exposure of the grotesquerie of suffering silence; Chaim Nachman Bialik's response to the infamous Kishinev pogrom was outrage against the *victims* who flee or hide, pretending that vengeance will come from God.

But there were always some who, like Rabbi Nachman, continued to uphold the psychological advantage of the man who believes in moral truth over the man whose trust is all in sociopolitical verities. The idea of faith, particularly when treated by writers outside the religious tradition, could only be associated with fools and madmen, since anyone more practical would see fate's malevolence for what it was. The figure of the schlemiel was employed to present the case of hope over despair, ironically, because the author retained his awareness of reality even if his character did not. The schlemiels are committed to Messianic truth, and if need be they can reinterpret, distort, or obviate immediate reality when it contradicts their ultimate ideal. Society finds them wanting, but according to the internal judgment of the story, their foolishness is redeemed. Rarely does the literary schlemiel rise to the heights achieved by the Bratzlaver's simple man, because rarely does the modern author share the great Rabbi's full-hearted conviction. More usually, the schlemiel remains the practical loser, winning only an ironic victory of interpretation.

The fool appears in many guises: on the battlefield he cries: "Stop shooting! Someone might, God forbid, lose an eye!" When studying Bible, he reads the text from his own changed historical perspective: "Naase venishma (Exodus 24:7). We will do and obey. A Jew is ready to promise anything!" He undercuts the worship of scholarship and the sanctity of learning which have been the pillars of his tradition, and when evil hurls itself against him with incomprehensible intensity, he says, "You have to be crazy not to believe in miracles."

In Yiddish fiction this fool is one version of the little man, the mainstay of Yiddish typology. Appropriately, *The Little Man* is the title of a novel by Mendele Mocher Sforim, the first appearance of which in 1864 is generally cited as the beginning of modern Yiddish prose. But Mendele's use of the term was pejorative; as his English translator accurately suggests, his little man is a "parasite." The schlemiel, quite to the contrary, is a little man sympathetically conceived and small only by sociological, not moral standards. He owns little, accomplishes little, and affects little in his environment. But as the impulse of schlemiel literature is to

invert all normal judgments, his littleness must impress us
with its size. Language—both Yiddish and English—is a
handicap here, since it encourages the equation of physical
importance with moral worth, as in the words *great*, *big*,
even *large*. When we try to make *little* swell into *great*, we
run into the danger of loving a character more than the language loves him, passing him off as being more worthy of
literary affection than he would be of actual love: the obvious danger of sentimentalizing. Schlemiel fiction and folklore avoid the danger, when they do, by making their inversions through a balanced humor that cuts simultaneously
into the character and into those belittling him. Even the
Bratzlaver's story is funny, and in spite of the deadly
earnestness of the following chapters, we ought to remember
that of the works themselves the first literary criterion is that
of laughter.

2. THE EVOLUTION OF A SATIRE

Mendele Mocher Sforim was one of the many writers in the history of literature who stoop to fiction to win the minds of masses, but are themselves won into the service of their weapons. The Haskalah, the Jewish Enlightenment, impelled him to write Yiddish fiction: Yiddish because even the poorly educated could read it, and fiction because even the poorly educated *would* read it. In a not unusual reversal, Mendele eventually abandoned the reformist platform that had kindled his missionary zeal, but his dedication to the craft of fiction steadily increased, and the challenge of forging an individual, supple prose style became the moving ambition of his life. The pseudonym, Mendele Mocher Sforim, or Mendele the Book Seller, was adopted by Sholom Abramovitch (1836–1917) when he wrote his first story, and remained his persona-signature in all subsequent Yiddish and Hebrew fictional writing.

As a young man, Mendele, then still Abramovitch, was attracted to the optimistic socioeconomic platform of the Haskalah. The Maskilim, encouraged by the progress of Jewish emancipation in France and Germany, proposed certain reforms which, if implemented by East European Jewish communities, would bring Jewry out of the shtetl, or

village community, and into the mainstream of Russian and
Polish life. They advocated widespread educational reform,
the teaching of secular subjects in addition to Torah, in-
struction in the local languages, the teaching of crafts, and
the establishment of trade schools. They encouraged adop-
tion of Western dress in place of the traditional black
kapote. The Jews were naturally afraid that these changes
would lead to assimilation and apostasy, but that is not our
present concern. The Maskilim were optimists. They main-
tained that the oppressed state of the Russian and Polish
Jewish populations could be altered by a collective act of
will. They preached self-help, convinced that a movement
outward by the Jewish enclave would be favorably received
by the political powers. They programmed for Eastern
European Jewry on the basis of Western European data.
This optimism reached its peak with the accession of Czar
Alexander II in 1855. It was followed by the most bitter
disillusionment when Alexander continued the reactionary
policy of his predecessor.

Mendele rode the forward-looking wave and felt the full
blast of disappointment when it crashed. A gifted satirist,
he began his literary career by exposing local vices and
follies: provincialism masking as tradition; exploitation
of the poor by the less poor; the private uses of public
monies. His work, like all satire, was based on the implied
existence of a moral and ethical social model, in this case
a cross between the traditional Jewish ethic and the Haskalah's progressive blueprint for reform. The deviants, or
objects of satire, were those who sinned in the terms of
Jewish (and universal) law, and those who ignored the
challenges of changing times. Teachers who beat their students because they were afraid to beat their wives were set
off against enlightened pedagogues who taught out of con-

viction and love. Community leaders lining their pockets at public expense (Stoneheart, Leech) were confronted by young idealists (Waker, Goodheart) whose concern was genuine communal advancement. Writing out of the conviction that more dedicated, wiser leaders could change the quality of Jewish life, Mendele poked malicious fun at those who seemed to be retarding its progress.

But the extreme poverty of Russian Jewry and its undiminishing vulnerability in the face of an anti-Semitic governmental policy made this line of chastening useless if not misleading. In 1873, in a social allegory called *Di kliatshe* (*The Nag*),[1] Mendele was among the first "Enlighteners" to expose the Haskalah formula to careful criticism. The nag, representing the Jewish masses, rejects the well-intentioned advice of Israel, member of the Society for the Prevention of Cruelty to Animals, the allegorical counterpart of the Haskalah. The Society submits its platform: cleanliness, modernization, and *education.* The nag says, "the dance does not precede the food"; no creature should have to prove its worth or earn its right to breathe and eat. Justice demands equal rights for all, and the claim of justice supersedes those of mercy or utilitarianism. Thus Mendele replaced the Haskalah's slogan—first education, then rights—with a slogan of his own: first the right to live, and then education. It seemed evident that unless the authorities sanctioned and encouraged "progress," the Jews would gain nothing by efforts on their own behalf.

The more Jews became the whipping boy of the Czarist and local governments, the harder it was for the satirist to jibe at their—by contrast—minor imperfections. Social satire is predicated on the possibility of social reform;

1. Mendele Mocher Sforim, *Di kliatshe* (Vilna, 1873). Translated by Moshe Spiegel as *The Nag* (New York, 1955).

where no reform is possible, the purpose of satire is blunted. Social satire can serve only those who control their own destinies, and whose actions affect their fate; Mendele's instrument was inappropriate for his readers, who seemed less and less in control of theirs.

The collapse of his social model posed yet another problem for Mendele the satirist. The ground of all satire is a social and ethical norm freely acknowledged by both reader and author. Fielding, for example, insists that "The only source of the true Ridiculous . . . is affectation . . . [which] proceeds from one of these two causes, vanity or hypocrisy; for as vanity puts us on affecting false characters, in order to purchase applause; so hypocrisy sets us on an endeavour to avoid censure, by concealing our vices under an appearance of their opposite virtues."[2] Implicit in the very vocabulary of the definition (affecting, concealing) is the concept of a stable social norm acknowledged by all, though transgressed by many. Fielding may be called a conservative satirist insofar as his criterion of integrity is based on the contemporary social norms: So, for example, Mrs. Slipslop aspires above and Lady Booby slips below her proper station, while Joseph and Fanny, by conforming to their given positions as they perceive them, represent the model of a stable society.

Swift's more radical satire sets up its models outside existing society, but still within the scope of human achievement. When, as in *A Modest Proposal*, two extremes are played off against each other to the demolition of both, the result is not satire, but irony.

In the worsening conditions of late nineteenth-century Russia, what could the Jewish satirist use as a social model?

2. Henry Fielding, in the Introduction to *Joseph Andrews*.

The Haskalah ideal of an ethical, progressive community was predicated on the rational assumption that better education, greater interaction with the European environment, and more productive economic occupations would lead to an improved existence. But casual and official anti-Semitism, particularly in their character of irrationality and unpredictability, belied this vision and made trust in reason seem to be the most unreasonable tenet of all. If the Haskalah model was rejected, there remained the model of the "status quo," the non-Jewish Russian bourgeoisie, including the intelligentsia. To uphold this model, the Jewish satirist would have had to reject his own community, its values as well as its past, just as the Jew who was drawn to this model by his own personal ambition had to reject his community in order to attain it. Mendele does not seem to have considered this alternative. Unlike Fielding, he could not accept the social structure as a norm to which all should adjust without first rejecting everything he hoped to achieve as a Jew. Nor could he, like Swift, use an ideal, rationally-conceived model: his readers might become as rational as the Houyhnhnms, but this would not prevent the local citizenry from slaughtering their women and children. His former model destroyed, and no substitute arising, Mendele gradually moved from satire to social allegory, to the novel of ideas, and to irony—a kind of satire in which the model is God, the unrealizable ideal of perfection, and in which the hopelessness of the existing conditions is pitted against the Messianic dream. Once the gap between reality and improvement is unbridgeable, the ideal to which the mind turns might as well be transcendental:

A Jew lives on faith and hope—and lucky is the man who has even this capital. But what of someone like me, whose intelligence has won him over, as the snake won over Eve, and who has already slipped into questioning and doubts? Such a man will suffer anguish and trouble by the ton. There are two alternatives open to you: either be a Jew like all Jews, live on faith, go with eyes shut wherever the wind may carry you, ask no questions, harbor no complaints, and live! Or else, if you want to be smart, reflective, and ask dead-end questions—this seems logical to you, but that doesn't; this appeals to you, but that is beyond the pale—well then, lay yourself out and die. Your complaints are mud, no one needs them. . . . Blind faith and hope are actually an asset for the Jew, they help him in his need, as sleeping-potion helps the stricken patient so that he should not feel the pain of the operation, else the pain would be too great to bear. There is no more miserable creature on earth than a Jew who begins to think.[3]

Folk humor had already produced a milder tradition of this kind of irony, and it remained for the writer to play it out in literary form. Although Mendele continued to depict the misery of Jews, he was less and less inclined to locate the fault with his people. And whereas he had previously seen only the bodies sunk in mud, he now began to make out the dim outlines of the foreheads touching heaven.

This shift of emphasis, spanning many years of writing, can be followed through a single work, *The Travels of Benjamin III* (Masoes Binyomin hashlishi), published in 1878. The exemplary social satire of the opening chapters gradually loses its bite; target of stinging laughter through the greater part of the book, the schlemiel victim, Benjamin, evolves into a schlemiel hero whose naïveté becomes a mockery of his mockers.

The Travels of Benjamin III starts out as a complex satire of provincialism and false aspirations. In Mendele's *Wishing Ring* the magical solution to the Jewish problem is sought in education. Here, two simpletons try to alter the

3. Mendele Mocher Sforim, "In a shturem tsayt" [In a time of storm], in *Ale Verk* (Warsaw, 1913), 9: 25.

fate of Jews along geographic lines, with faith as their compass and the beggar's pouch for sustenance. According to them, they are merely symptomatic: "What do all the rest of the Jews do? This week some go begging from door to door, and next week their benefactors come begging at their door. It's the Jewish way of life."

The book is introduced by the persona, Mendele the Book Seller, who explains how and why he is bringing this material to the attention of his readers:

Last year the English and German newspapers were filled with accounts of the wonderful journey undertaken by Benjamin, a certain Polish Jew, to some distant lands in the East. "Just think" —they marvelled—"a Jew, a Polish Jew, without weapons or means of transportation, with only a sack on his shoulders and a philacteries-bag under his arm, has visited countries that even renowned British explorers have been unable to reach! Obviously, this was not achieved by merely human powers, but by a power that the intelligence cannot grasp; that is to say, the intelligence is as powerless to grasp it as the power itself is unintelligible. In any case, however it came about, the world has Benjamin to thank for the marvels, the great wonders that were revealed through him, and which have quite altered the map of the world.[4]

The saga then follows Benjamin III and his hen-pecked companion, aptly nicknamed Senderl the Housewife, in their quest for the Red Jews, the remnant of the ten lost tribes of Israel, who, in legend and lore, inhabit the lands behind the River Sambatyon. At least three strands of satire are discernible: as the story echoes *Don Quixote,* it parodies travelogue and adventure fiction, in a style that may best be called mock kheder.

4. Mendele Mocher Sforim, *Masoes Binyomin hashlishi* (Vilna, 1878). Translated by Moshe Spiegel as *The Travels and Adventures of Benjamin III* (New York, 1949). I have relied heavily on this translation, but with occasional modifications where the translator has been too free. The quotations are from pages 16–17, 116, 117, 118, and 123.

Part of the book's humor derives from the identification of Benjamin III with the Knight of La Mancha and of Senderl the Housewife with Sancho Panza. The resemblance between the Eastern European bumpkins and the famous adventurers of Spain (which country in Cervantes' time had but recently become *judenrein*) adds poignancy to the satire. For is it not bitterly ironic that the Jews after 250 years of self-disciplined exile should find this particular Spanish dybbuk in their midst? And Benjamin is merely the parody of a parody; whereas Quixote is clearly an aristocratic dreamer, Benjamin is a beggar, a pauper representing the whole society of paupers. Yet, the similarities between both sets of travelers also lend the book a certain universalism; lowly Yiddish, the jargon of the masses, has produced a companion to the great Spanish masterpiece. The Spanish echo makes the satire at one and the same time more familiar and more formidable, not unlike the ambiguous effect of Ulysses dwarfing Bloom. The single frame device of evoking *Don Quixote* introduces an ironic mixture of pride and shame.

The book is also a mock travelogue, presumably in the tradition of the Jewish explorers, but actually more reminiscent of "bobe mayses," the folktales and legends that were accepted by the simpleminded as truth. The early explorer Benjamin of Tudela (Benjamin I) was a twelfthcentury Spanish Jew who traveled widely around the Mediterranean and the Near East, looking for Jewish communities and writing detailed accounts of those he found. Nearer to the present, Jacob I. Benjamin, or Benjamin II, spent eight years in Asia and Africa (1846–55) and three years in America (1859–62), and his published reports were fresh in the minds of Mendele and his readers. Benjamin III, our hypothetical hero, was placed in this illustrious line just as Crusoe and Gulliver pretended to be true explorers in their time. It is doubtful whether any reader was ever meant to take literally Mendele's fiction, since the very title is clearly satirical and the style is much too inflated for factual reportage, more so than either Defoe's or Swift's.

Predictably, Benjamin III's travels do not take him any farther than the nearest town, where people live in tall buildings "as an expression of their heavenly striving." In his later Hebrew version of the book, Mendele includes an afterword that predicts a second journey for Benjamin and Senderl in the company of the recently founded Lovers of Zion movement. The Lovers of Zion (Chibey Zion) Societies came into being between the writing of the Yiddish book and Mendele's own Hebrew "translation," and he evidently saw in the efforts of these early Zionist groups an uncanny resemblance to his own literary schlemiels. Whatever anti-Zionist sentiment the book contains is directed at the early sentimentalists, not the political activists of the end of the century.

But even as it mocks the heroes' efforts to change their luck by changing their place, the book also exposes the credulity and insularity of shtetl Jews who are content to remain as they are. The legends and superstitions that developed during the centuries of shtetl life reflected the distortion of its inhabitants. Benjamin III, inveterate reader of these tales, suffers from an inflamed, chimera-prone imagination, like Quixote whose brain was fired by the romances of his day. In acting out the legends, Benjamin demonstrates his foolishness, but also the folly of those around him. The book ridicules the absurd romanticism of the protagonist, but it is no kinder to the pragmatists who exploit this folly and so reveal their more culpable sins.

Certain sections of the narrative, including the introduction, are written in the Yiddish equivalent of the mock epic:
the mock kheder style. The Bible and commentaries, being
the only Jewish counterpart to the epics, were taught by
means of a Hebrew-Yiddish transposition—"*berayshis*, in
the beginning, *boro elohim*, God created." The narrator of
The Travels of Benjamin III uses this Hebrew-Yiddish cross
movement as Pope used epic language and imagery to in-
flate the style and inevitably deflate events so described.

The blending of these three devices—parallels with *Don
Quixote*, parodies of travel and folklore, projection of
kheder style on mundane matters—emphasizes the gulf
between the great past of Spain, cosmopolitan Jewries, Bible
and commentaries, and the puny present of poverty, isolation, and ignorance. Benjamin is the embodiment of that
puny present, at least as long as he moves within the Jewish
milieu. When at the book's conclusion he moves out into the
openly hostile gentile world, not by choice, but by coercion,
he ceases to be simply the goat and becomes the subject of a
compassionate irony. The heroic potential of the schlemiel
is then revealed.

In the opening chapter of the *Travels*, the "politicians"
of the fictional shtetl, Tuneyadevke, assembled in the local
bathhouse, debate the stability of Rothschild's millions and
the progress of European politics since the Crimean War.
From various subcommittees, arguments are passed on till
they reach the highest bench in the bathhouse,

and there, at the full plenary gathering of local big-wigs, they are
decided once and for all and irrevocably, so that if all the rulers of
the East and the West were to view the verdict with disfavor and
ask for reconsideration, it wouldn't do them any good. The Turks
were almost sacrificed once at such a palaver—who knows what
would have become of them had several right-minded citizens not

defended their interest? Rothschild, God help him, almost lost some ten to fifteen million rubles there. But luckily, several weeks later, when the bathhouse statesmen were in high spirits, he was suddenly granted a clear gain of a hundred million rubles!

Thus the politicoeconomic impotence of the shtetl is translated into linguistic aggression. Language is Tuneyadevke's forte, Talmudic proofs and counterproofs are its chief commodity, and the pilpulists on the highest judgmental bench are able to replace the world's reality by the reality of their argumentative concern. The map of Europe becomes just another Talmud folio, the Turk and Aunt Vita (Queen Victoria) simply another Reuben and Simon, whose fate will be decided not, as the world might imagine, by force of arms, strength of alliances, power of technology, skill of generals, but by the shrewd arguments of Tuneyadevke's disembodied mind. The author pretends to respect the ultimate seriousness of the deliberations—"Rothschild, *God bless him*"; "But *luckily*, several weeks later"—leaving the reader to laugh at the discrepancy between hard reality and Tuneyadevke's verbal version of it.

Even at this point, where the absurdity of the deluded kingmakers is most apparent, the satire is mitigated by a contradictory note of, let us say, wonderment. The residents of this backwater shtetl are "jolly paupers, happy beggars, wild men of faith." The bathhouse debate is followed by a conversation with a typical *luftmensch*, a dreamer, whose poverty and lack of opportunity are matched by his absolute belief in God's friendship. Although the theme of the happy paupers is usually associated with Sholom Aleichem, we see that Mendele, in this ambivalent presentation of weakness, has already introduced the type. These disenfranchized Jews who managed the fortunes of Rothschild while lacking the price of bread, were fortunate; their

salutory delusion softened the hardships of daily living.
Could the Jews have aspired to control or influence their
environment, their self-deception—what Mendele has
called the sleeping potion—would have been wasteful foolishness. But if aspiration was itself the illusion, then illusion became the only recourse. It alone could liberate,
freeing the community from despair, permitting at least
the power of thought and the freedom of speech.

A second and later discussion of politics in the prayerhouse of the larger town of Teterivke is marked by more
heated polemic. The immediate topic is the feasibility of
Benjamin and Senderl's trip to the east, but this spills over
into well-worn considerations of European alliances, each
member of the prayerhouse debating club supporting his
usual side. Once again, the fun is at the expense of the Jews
who kibitz at the sidelines of political life but don't try to
affect it in any direct way. The object of the satire is not
merely Jewish inaction and innocence, but the affectation—
in Fielding's sense—of an omniscience and power they lack.
At this point, Mendele is still within the general convention
of satire, and Benjamin's travels are but a symptom of his
society's ills.

The shift of emphasis occurs in the final three chapters
when Benjamin and Senderl are waylaid by *khappers*, kid-
nappers who abduct Jewish boys and gullible strangers and
sell them into czarist army service. That our protagonists
suffer this ignoble fate is further proof of their childlike
innocence and of the terrible power of those who prey on
the simpleminded. But once the two simpletons are forced
into the army and are virtually captive in the czarist service,
the satire reverses its target:

Looking at them [Benjamin and Senderl] you would think it was all
an act, that two Jews had turned up in disguise and were poking fun

at the soldiers, imitating their gestures, and demonstrating publicly how silly they really were with all their kit and caboodle.

The erstwhile fools are now touchstones of a foolishness greater than their own. In their milieu, fools; yet their folly is wisdom when compared with the more radical stupidity-in-power of their captors. Senderl tries to be a proper soldier, but Benjamin rebukes him sharply:

> "What good are we to them, or they to us? Honestly, Senderl, tell me as you are a Jew, were the enemy, God forbid, to appear— would the two of us be able to stop him? And if you warned him a thousand times: 'Go away, or I'll go pow! pow! pow!' would he pay any attention to you? Of course not. He'd grab hold of you, and you'd be lucky to get out of his clutches alive."

As in the pacifist jokes, the incomprehension of the Jew here reveals the incomprehensibility of war.

Benjamin engineers their escape from the army camp, but predictably they are apprehended. The two "soldiers" are then court-martialed, and Benjamin speaks in their defense at the trial. After describing their forced induction into army service, he introduces his final plea:

> "We would like to inform you that we don't know a thing about waging war, we never did know, and we never want to know. We are, praise be to God, married men, and our thoughts are devoted to other things. We can't waste our time on these matters, they don't even concern us."

The team of doctors and officers can barely conceal its laughter. The medical officer taps his forehead to indicate a screw loose. The two Jews are discharged from the army, to their mutual benefit, and so the book ends.

But the verdict of the officers does not reflect the verdict of the reader, and it is the officers, in their mockery, who are mocked. At the story level, Benjamin achieves his goal: he

wins release from captivity. Thematically, his passivism
becomes a pacifism exposing the absurdity of married men
who *do* engage in the foolishness of war.

The political impotence of the Jew, his ignorance and
childlike conceptions of power, have been exposed and ridiculed throughout the book. Yet when Benjamin becomes
the actual victim of a power system he has hitherto ignored,
instead of pushing the satire farther to its logical conclusion,
showing that ignorance will lead to victimization and even
destruction, Mendele redirects the satiric machinery and
vindicates his schlemiel. The laughter that Benjamin evokes
in the army environment is enough to make Mendele come
to his defense. Or, to put it differently, faced with the alternative of real power, which means in these circumstances,
conformity to the gentile status quo, militarism and anti-
Semitism, Benjamin's foolishness seems a blessing in disguise, a way of remaining innocent in action as well as in
thought.

The book ends most abruptly. Mendele's later Hebrew
postscript is very brief and does not significantly alter or
resolve the unfinished nature of the story. Perhaps the
author was himself surprised by the turn his narrative had
taken. After revealing Benjamin's absolute vulnerability,
and after elevating that vulnerability—albeit ironically—
to a positive value, there could be little point in reverting
to the earlier Jewish milieu and earlier satiric sallies. So
the book ends with the heroes having passed through both
environments and facing only their fantasy.

Benjamin is a schlemiel: a victim not so much of bad
luck as of miserable circumstance. His masculinity, like
that of all literary schlemiels, is undermined by his wife at
home and by the aggression of the environment. For the
better part of the book he embodies all the psychological

and historical weaknesses the author is ridiculing, and Mendele spares no comic or satiric devices in holding these weaknesses up to view. Then, almost without warning, Benjamin in his simplicity becomes a serious moral alternative to the organized evil that would destroy him. He has not evolved in any way. A satire is not a bildungsroman. He is not suddenly a Shakespearean fool, unmasking the widespread folly that men call wisdom, or worship as power. Only the point of view has changed: from the satire that exposes, attacks, and pleads for reform, to irony which is more tolerant if less optimistic. The traditional Western protagonist is heroic insofar as he attempts to change reality. The schlemiel becomes a hero when real action is impossible and reaction remains the only way a man can define himself. As long as he moves among choices, the schlemiel is derided for his failures to choose wisely. Once the environment is seen as unalterable—and evil—his stance must be accepted as a stand or the possibilities of "heroism" are lost to him altogether.

In this respect, the schlemiel differs from most anti-heroes who are characterized—as the term accurately implies—by means of negative definition. The schlemiel is not a hero manqué, but a challenge to the whole accepted notion of heroism. He responds not to the question of whether classical heroism is still possible, but of whether it was ever desirable. Ben Zoma says (*Pirke avoth*, IV, 1) "Who is mighty? He who subdues his urges." The schlemiel is mighty in that he subdues his urge to be a hero.

What can be claimed for Benjamin? He accepts his foolishness in both the local and cosmic dramas, forfeiting not only the Christian's pride before God, but even that cardinal Western virtue of pride in oneself. He retains only the sense of his own human worth. A later schlemiel, Malamud's

Fidelman, steals his own copy of Titian's Venus rather than the original, because it is his, worse but more personal.

The evolution from satire to irony in *The Travels of Benjamin III* corresponds to the shift of the schlemiel from object to subject against the backdrop of ever-worsening environmental pressures. The schlemiel, who had been around in the folk culture, became a potential hero when the ordinary Jew could no longer be regarded as master of his fate, and when the artist had therefore to move into a realm beyond satire and out of its reach.

3. IRONIC BALANCE FOR PSYCHIC SURVIVAL

Sholom Aleichem (1859–1916) established a genealogy of modern Yiddish letters when he designated Mendele Mocher Sforim as the *zeyde,* the grandfather. The title with its implied kinship was accepted by Mendele and ratified by public consent although the two men were barely a generation apart. Even as it acknowledges the resemblances between the two writers, the appellation emphasizes the relative distance between them. In developing the concept of the schlemiel, as in his writing generally, Sholom Aleichem is directly indebted to Mendele but plays astonishing variations on the master's theme.

The Soviet Yiddish critic, N. Oislender, distinguishes Sholom Aleichem's environment from Mendele's, pointing out that the upheavals in Russia of the 1880s brought about changes that a two-hundred-year period would not formerly have wrought.[1]

The Haskalah, which lost face in the 1870s, was totally discredited in the 1880s, leaving in its wake thousands of

1. N. Oislender, "Der yunger Sholom Aleychem un zayn roman, *Stempenyu*" [Young Sholom Aleichem and his novel, *Stempenyu*]. In *Shriftn fun der Katedre far Yidisher Kultur bay der Alukrainisher Visnshaftlekher Akademie*, Kiev, 1 (1928): 13, passim.

newly enlightened Jews who could no longer return to the
old forms of life and who thrashed about looking for new
philosophic and practical directions. Pogroms and hostile
edicts directed especially against them made the dislocation
of Jewish communities more severe than in the rest of Russia. The percentage of Jewish emigration was three times
greater than that of other Russian minorities, reflecting the
harsher pressures driving them to leave and the greater
turmoil this emigration itself then caused in the affected
communities.[2] At first there seems to have been a tacit agree-
ment among Jewish writers to keep silent on the pogrom
subject, though the profound unease and insecurity of the
times appears in their work in transmuted form.

In reaction to widespread poverty and unrest, Sholom
Aleichem felt that the wholesale criticism of Jewish life
ought to give way to the idealization of certain of its admirable tendencies and types. Some earnest readers attacked
Sholom Aleichem's first humorous sketches, insisting that
a Jewish writer ought to be producing more serious stuff.
They, at least, understood that humor, unlike satire, is an
enemy of "progress" because it purges through laughter
rather than inciting to change. But although Sholom Aleichem was certainly aware of Jewish shortcomings, he was
correspondingly pessimistic about all the suggested rem-
edies for improvement. He was, for example, a warm sup-
porter of the Zionist cause, but did not ever seem to believe
in its efficacy. In certain moments his characters can refer
to Zionism (tsionism) as cynicism (tsinism), and other
ideological trends fare even worse.

Alone among nineteenth-century authors, he wrote a

2. S. Ettinger, "The Jews at the Outbreak of the Revolution," in *The
Jews in Soviet Russia since 1917*, ed. Lionel Kochan (Oxford, 1970),
p. 21.

novel of fathers and sons in which the point of view is that
of the parent generation; that the novel is actually about
father and daughters, with the confrontations arising between father and sons-in-law, ensures the comic tone that
effectively pulls the teeth of all revolutionary stands. No
matter how limited Tevye the Dairyman may be, he is
nobler and certainly far more interesting to the author
than any of his children. No matter how imperfect his culture, it is deemed incomparably wiser than their proposed
alternatives. The humor of Sholom Aleichem, usually described as optimistic, is the result of a profoundly gloomy
appraisal of Jewish life in Eastern Europe and a conscious
decision to ease its sufferings. Almost all those who represent new directions in his work—the modern set in the
story "Cnards," who mock the superstitions of their back-
woods shtetl; Pertchik the revolutionary of "Hodel"; the
mother who feels compelled to get her son into the state
high school in the story "Gymnasium"—all are reproached
for their attempt by the internal verdict of the fiction in
which they figure. Emancipation to his characters means
escape from the confinement of stultifying Jewish practice
and belief. But to Sholom Aleichem, its precondition, the
abandonment of the civilizing Jewish structure, was a
ridiculous price to pay, especially since the real prospect of
"emancipation" was chimerical. The only ones who may
successfully challenge the tradition are the children, whose
alternative is not another society, but the escape to nature or
to art. The boy who would rather play with a calf than sit
in the house of study, or the boy who would rather play the
fiddle than adjust to the machinery of shtetl stratification,
are the sole vehicles through whom the evils of shtetl life
may safely be criticized. And only because they stand
against all and any society, because they are more "unreal-

istic" than even their elders, and better still at denying the tyrannical crucible in which their tortured destiny is being forged.

Sholom Aleichem conceived of his writing as a solace for people whose situation was so ineluctably unpleasant that they might as well laugh. The Jews of his works are a kind of schlemiel people, powerless and unlucky, but psychologically, or, as one used to say, spiritually, the victors in defeat.[3] Maurice Samuel has explained this technique as follows:

We must be careful to understand the nature of Sholom Aleichem's laughter. It is more than a therapeutic resistance to the destructive frustrations and humiliations of the Exile. It was the application of a fantastic technique that the Jews had developed over the ages . . . to counter the torments and discriminations to which they were continuously subjected. It was a technique of avoidance and sublimation; also a technique of theoretical reversal. They had found the trick of converting disaster into a verbal triumph, applying a sort of Talmudic ingenuity of interpretation to events they could not handle in their reality. They turned the tables on their adversaries dialectically, and though their physical disadvantages were not diminished thereby, nor the external situation changed one whit, they emerged with a feeling of victory.[4]

This technique may be demonstrated in the following story:

In 1902 Sholom Aleichem wrote "Dreyfus in Kasrilevke," an account of the second trial from the standpoint of a Ukrainian shtetl. Kasrilevke, the town of jolly paupers, is Sholom Aleichem's fictional equivalent for "any one of a hundred Jewish or half-Jewish centres in old White Russia,"[5] and it serves as the locale in many of his works. In

3. The term is introduced in a discussion of masochistic elements in Jewish jokes, in Theodor Reik's *Jewish Wit* (New York, 1962).

4. Maurice Samuel, "The Tribune of the Golus," *Jewish Book Annual*, 25 (1967–68) : 54.

5. Maurice Samuel, *The World of Sholom Aleichem* (New York, 1956), p. 26.

this brief story, Zaidl, the only Kasrilevkite to subscribe to a daily paper, becomes the sole communication medium for the news-hungry inhabitants. Each morning they besiege the post office, waiting for Zaidl to pick up his mail and read aloud the most recent events of the trial. Tension mounts, and on the morning when the verdict is expected, the atmosphere is charged. The conclusion of the story reads:

> When Yarmo, the janitor, unlocked the gates of the post office they all rushed inside at once. Yarmo became very angry—he'd show them who was boss here—and he drove them, with curses and insults, out into the street. And there in the street they waited and waited for Zaidl to make his appearance. And when at last Zaidl appeared, and when at last he picked up the paper and read aloud to them that nice passage about Dreyfus, there arose such a roar, such a protest, that the very heavens must have split. And this protest was not against the judge who had judged so badly; it was not against the generals who had sworn so falsely nor against the Frenchmen who had covered themselves with so much shame. No, this protest was against Zaidl, who read to them.
>
> "It can't be!" Kasrilevke screamed with one voice. "It can't be! The heavens and the earth have promised that the truth must always come out on top, just as oil comes to the top of water! What will you tell us next? What lies? What stories?"
>
> "Idiots!" shouted poor Zaidl with all the strength of his lungs, and he pushed the newspaper right into their faces. "Here! See what it says here in the paper!"
>
> "Paper!" cried Kasrilevke. "Paper! And if you stood here with one foot in heaven and one foot on earth we still wouldn't believe you. Such things cannot be! No, this cannot be! It cannot be! It cannot be!"
>
> Well, and who was right?[6]

Here too, as in the political discussions of Mendele's bath-

6. Sholom Aleichem, "Dreyfus in Kasrilevke," trans. Hilda Abel, in *A Treasury of Yiddish Stories*, ed. Irving Howe and Eliezer Greenberg (New York, 1953).

house philosophers, the disputants are impervious to the
immediate indignities and sublimate their personal humiliation in the political arena. Here, too, the oppressed replace
the world's reality with the reality of their argumentative
concern. But the Sholom Aleichem story equates the Jews'
far-sightedness with faith, whereas Mendele treats it simply
as folly. For Mendele, who was aiming his satire at Tuneyadevke and Teterivke, a hard-headed confrontation with
reality was the first desirable step on the road to emancipation. For Sholom Aleichem, who was consoling, or better
still, cajoling Kasrilevke, reality was the last enemy to be
conquered. Dreyfus in Kasrilevke is judged by God's law;
and is God's truth to be sacrificed for journalism? The tone
of the passage, and the concluding question in particular,
throw the weight of sympathy entirely to the side of the
dreamers. Men like Zaidl, among them, presumably, the
reader, who place their trust in objective reality, are bound
to the temporal, and hence their truth is but temporary. The
inhabitants of Kasrilevke live by the prophetic law. To them
the "ought" is more real than the "is," and their truth,
though uncorroborated by immediate evidence, is inde-
structible. The concluding question challenges the reader's
pragmatism from the point of view of the shtetl's wild faith.
It asks whether trust in the newspaper is any more rational
in the long run than Kasrilevke's trust in divine justice.
From the timeless perspective of God, all will ultimately
receive fair judgment; and in this case, as the author hints,
even the earthly verdict was eventually reversed.

Here, as in most of his fiction, Sholom Aleichem's treat-
ment of the schlemiel is ironic, not satiric. Irony, generally
defined as "a device by which a writer expresses a meaning
contradictory to the stated or ostensible one," has one statement supporting two meanings, the literal, or primary, and

the implied, or secondary. The tone of the irony will be determined by the relative weight of both meanings: if the inversion is total and the primary is wholly contradicted by the secondary, the irony is heavy; it then borders on sarcasm, in which the primary meaning is extinct; if the primary is only partly qualified, the irony is light.

The classic expression of Yiddish irony is the saying:

אתה בחרתנו מכל העמים: וואָס האָסטו
געוואָלט פון דיין פאָלק ישראל?

[Thou hast chosen us from among the nations—why did you have to pick on the Jews?] Although this is a Yiddish saying, the first part is Hebrew: a quotation of one of the most prominent phrases of the daily prayers which expresses a central precept of Judaism. The Yiddish question then draws attention to the ironic implications of the quoted phrase. The proverb is in two parts, affirmation and question. The affirmation is in the sacred language, the jibe in the vernacular. The form is dramatic, and the challenge, forcing on the affirmation a meaning contradictory to the ostensible one, is in the traditional Jewish form of aggression, a question.

Since the saying is presented as point-counterpoint in two voices, its very structure obviates the possibility of a total inversion. The question does not eliminate the primary meaning that prompted it; it introduces ambiguity where absolute clarity once prevailed.

Yiddish irony often takes the form of statement and counterstatement, to the same effect. The dialectic was especially fertile in the vital field of economic theory: "Rich and poor, both lie in the ground together; but on the ground the rich lie more comfortably." "Money is dirt; but is dirt money?" "If you're poor, you're dead: but being rich doesn't make you alive." No sacred text was immune from undercutting: "Imru L'adonoy, speak to the Lord; and talk to the wall."[7]

Two voices on two levels offer contradictory interpretations of the same phenomenon: absolute faith in the holy tongue, in Biblical majesty, against absolute skepticism, in the interrogative voice, in marketplace Yiddish. Meaning and countermeaning lock horns. The primary meaning is challenged by the secondary, but the final authority of the primary is never eradicated. As in the saying, "God will provide—if only God would provide until he provides," faith is punctured but not sunk. This appears to be the prevalent form of Yiddish irony, and the kind from which the schlemiel derives.

Yiddish proverbs include variously weighted ironies. "He who lies on the ground cannot fall," or "Dying young is a boon in old age" are two of the many examples of meiosis where the redemptive undertow is lacking.[8] Black humor, or galgen-humor, is heavily indebted to this technique of unpleasant understatement of fact. And there are also examples of heavy irony: "If psalms were a cure, they'd be sold at the drugstore," in which the skeptical countermeaning demolishes the implied position of faith.

But schlemiel humor is based on the same polarization

7. Some of the wittiest of these puns are, as might be expected, untranslatable: An eyshes khayil—zi iz antlofn mit an ofitsir [A woman of valor (in Hebrew also soldier)—she has run off with an officer].

8. An interesting theory about this kind of proverb is presented by N. Oislender, *Gruntshtrikhn fun yidishn realism* [Basic characteristics of Yiddish realism] (Vilna, 1928), pp. 24–25. Oislender suggests that the Messianic ideology began to give way to a more realistic weltanschauung, and that the proverbs reflect the rise of realism over idealism. The examples of meiosis bear out Oislender's theory, but the main concern of this chapter is the irony of those proverbs in which the struggle between realism and idealism is still ongoing.

of faith and fact that we find in the proverb on the chosen people, and is resolved on the same side. In "Dreyfus in Kasrilevke," Sholom Aleichem draws our attention to the discrepancy between the ideal and the actual, but as its primary statement is one of skepticism, the counterstatement is one of faith. Again a question is asked, "Well, and who was right?" with the aggression now aimed at the scoffers. The Sholom Aleichem story contains a double irony. The ideal pits itself against reality but is finally vindicated by that same reality. Were Dreyfus not finally acquitted in the human courts of law, the schlemiel insistence on God's justice would have been less convincing.

Sholom Aleichem's most exhaustive study of the schlemiel is Menahem Mendl, a luftmensch, or a schlemiel in his economic dimension.

Menahem Mendl, an epistolary novel written between 1892 and 1913,[9] consists of an exchange of letters between Menahem Mendl, the errant husband, and Sheyne Sheyndl of Kasrilevke, the steady wife. The two voices of the ironic proverbs are here expanded into two full-blown characters, one voicing trust and optimism, the other convinced that "Kreplach in a dream are not kreplach, but a dream."

Menahem Mendl aspires to great wealth, yet fails successively at a long list of occupations: as an investor in stocks, in bonds, in commodities; as a stockbroker, sugarbroker, factorer; as an agent for houses, manors and estates, timber forests, small factories; as a journalist, marriage

9. For a detailed bibliographical account of the individual episodes as they appeared in various Yiddish periodicals see Max Erik, "Oyf di shpurn fun Menakhem Mendl" [On the trail of Menahem Mendl] *Bikhervelt* (Warsaw, 1928), 1: 3–10; 2: 13–17. A study by Khone Shmeruk, "Vegn Sholem Aleykhems letster Menakhem Mendl serie," *Di goldene keyt* (Tel Aviv) 56 (1966) : 22–27, discusses the later letters which were excluded from Sholom Aleichem's final edition of the work. The discussion here is limited to the book as an independent work of fiction.

broker, insurance agent. Sheyne Sheyndl, reinforced by the prodding and proverbs of her mother, upholds the pragmatic standard, urging her husband to sell and come home. But she is bested—just as Zaidl is bested—by the appeal to faith, and single-minded trust. As in the proverbs just referred to, weight of emphasis seesaws between Menahem Mendl's credulity and Sheyne Sheyndl's practicality. The seesaw comes down eventually on the side of the dreamer; by the end of the series of letters, only Menahem Mendl's are given, a hint that the argument has been decisively won, or at least that the husband is the more entertaining combatant.

In an earlier dialogue of this kind, the conversation between Chanticleer and Pertelote in Chaucer's "Nun's Priest's Tale," there is simply no appeal against the wife's prescription of "digestyves and laxatyves." Chanticleer's romantic idealism, there associated with his vanity, must be purged. Applying a model of rational behavior to which neither Chanticleer nor Pertelote conforms, Chaucer plays off husband against wife, using Pertelote's matter-of-factness to puncture the inflated singer, and, to a lesser degree, Pertelote's own brittle self-assuredness to bring laughter upon herself. But the husband is clearly the loser.

Menahem Mendl is similarly conceived, except that the author's point of view, based on his personal experience, is more tightly merged with the hero's.

Sholom Aleichem had lost his own fortune (plus the fortune of his in-laws) on the Kiev stock exchange, and his own subsequent hustling for bread was a typical experience of the Jew. A modern historian has estimated that "in many communities up to 40 percent of the entire Jewish population consisted of families of so-called *Luftmenschen,* that is persons without any particular skills, capital, or specific occupations."[10] In those desperate times Sholom Aleichem did not believe one could properly chastise the luftmensch for living on air, since there was no more nourishing substance available. So the practical voice of Sheyne Sheyndl is drowned out by the passionate daydreaming of her husband. Menahem Mendl, unlike Chanticleer, is never forced to confront the fox, the harsh danger of his real surroundings. In spite of an unbroken record of failures, the hero succeeds in his determined hope; Menahem Mendl wrests victory from defeat not by any tangible achievement of his purposes, but simply through his continuing capacity to dream. It is as though the schlemiel were inverting the famous dictum of Theodore Herzl, and saying, "If you will it, it *is* a dream."

Here again the schlemiel's humor is the product of an antirational bias which inverts the rational model underlying so much of English humor, substituting for it a messianic or idealist model instead. In the words of *The Enchanted Tailor*, "The hungrier I am, the louder I sing."

The characteristic features of the schlemiel are exemplified in the figure of Menahem Mendl: his masculinity is never considered; it is thoroughly extinct. The traditional male virtues such as strength, courage, pride, fortitude, are prominent only in their absence. Wife treats husband like an overgrown, overly fanciful child. Behind the wife stands the more formidable mother-in-law, and together they could undermine the virility of an Ajax. This is but a sample of the barrage that assults our hero:

"A sick man will get better, a drunkard will grow sober, a black man will turn white, but a fool will stay a fool."

"If you don't have fingers, you can't thumb your nose."

10. Salo Baron, *The Russian Jew Under Tsars and Soviets* (New York, 1964), p. 114.

"A shlimazl falls on the grass and breaks his nose."

"Remember what I say, Mendl, they'll bring you home either in chains or in a winding sheet, as you deserve."

The familial pattern of subjugation and humiliation is a sociopolitical model in miniature. Like all Russian Jews, with the exception of a privileged few, Menahem Mendl was confined to the Pale of Settlement and could not legally trade in Yehupetz (Kiev) without a permit.

When you write to me, write to me in Boiberik, because I'm not allowed to be in Yehupetz. So I keep moving all day along Creshtchatek Street near the exchange, and in the evening I hop down to Boiberik.[11]

His vulnerability makes him equally susceptible to subtler social pressures. In the ice-cream parlor of Odessa, a hovering waiter must be appeased by successive orders of ice cream, and the resultant intestinal malfunctioning then makes it impossible to visit the ice-cream parlor. Even in the synagogue, since he is an outsider and a provincial, Menahem Mendl is rebuked for praying too loudly.

But like the characteristic schlemiel, though he fails in action, he scores in his reactions. In a not untypical letter, Menahem Mendl informs his wife that although his dealings in houses have come to nought, by a lucky coincidence he is now an agent for estates. He was aroused at midnight by the landlady of his rooming house frantically giving warning of the approach of police, whose practice was to raid the area in search of unlicensed Jews. Hiding in the attic, uncomfortably flat on his stomach, he enters into whispered conversation with a fellow fugitive, who suddenly remembers that he has left his papers under his

11. Sholom Aleichem, *Menakhem Mendl* (Warsaw, 1909). Translations are my own. The book has been translated into English as *The Adventures of Menahem-Mendl* by Tamara Kahana (New York, 1969).

pillow. The inevitable question, "What papers?" introduces the subject of estates, of which the man in hiding is, as it happens, an agent. By the end of their night of concealment they are in partnership together, and Menahem Mendl is enthusiastically hopeful once again. Oh yes, he adds in a postscript, the whole escapade was a false alarm. A neighbor mistakenly hammered a warning on the windows, but wasn't that a lucky error!

The situation is grotesque. Kafka's heroes find themselves challenged by the same irrational and impersonal forces of hostility that assault the individual without ever confronting him in his individuality. But whereas Kafka's heroes—Gregor, K, Karl Rossman—accept, or internalize, the hostile outside order, struggling to conform to it if they are still part of its machinery, or to adjust to it if they have slipped from grace and face a challenging authority, Sholom Aleichem's heroes do not confuse their own ethos with that of the environment. Menahem Mendl is fully prepared for a "pounding at the window," and his instinctive response is to flee and hide. But he is so completely dissociated from his enemy, real or imagined, that his own course of life goes on, uninterrupted, in fact even stimulated, by the external danger. Kafka's heroes are themselves a part of the universal horror confronting them. Sholom Aleichem's heroes are confronted by horror, but within a universe of meaning.

Thus Sholom Aleichem's schlemiel, for all his simplicity, or naïveté, or weakness, or dreaminess, or predisposition for misfortune, or whatever tendency it is that makes him a schlemiel, retains a very firm sense of his distinct self. His sense of personal identity and worth is not seriously disrupted by the bombardment of environmental harrassments. The schlemiel represents the triumph of identity despite the failure of circumstance.

The full power of that identity is communicated to the reader by having the schlemiel tell the story in his own voice. Sholom Aleichem generally employs the technique of monologue, of which the epistolary form is but a variation, to convey the rhythms and nuances of character, and to underscore the extent to which language itself is the schlemiel's manipulative tool. Through language the schlemiel reinterprets events to conform to his own vision, and thereby controls them, much as the child learns to control the environment by naming it. One need only read Menahem Mendl's joyous, and incomprehensible, explanation of the stock market to appreciate how proficient handling of language can become a substitute for proficient commerce.

Moreover, the richness of the language in some way compensates for the poverty it describes. There is in the style an overabundance of nouns, sayings, explanations, in apposition. Even the names are multiple: Menahem Mendl; Sheyne Sheyndl, or Meir-Motl-Moshe-Meir's. To communicate the simple information that he is out of the "timber business," Menahem Mendl writes:

> This is to let you know that the forests have turned into a barren steppe. *Loy Dubim Veloy Yar* [a Hebrew expression meaning "there are no bears, there is no forest"], there is no forest, there are no trees, there is no river, it's a hopeless case! It was useless to stir up trouble for others and for myself. I strained my feet for nothing; I wore out my boots over nothing. I realized, my dear wife, that forests are not for me, and dealing with such splendid liars is beyond me. They can dream up a marketplace in heaven, and arrange for you to fall into the lower depths!

The exuberant self-indulgence of this description of disaster takes the sting out of the failure itself. This is not what Maurice Samuel has called "theoretical reversal," although Sholom Aleichem's characters, especially Tevye the Dairyman, often achieve spectacular verbal triumphs through wit. Here, by the very lushness of his account, Menahem Mendl transforms the event of failure into a declamatory success. If we measure life, and language, by intensities of experience rather than by objective tests of achievement, the schlemiel is no loser. Enough is always too much in *Menahem Mendl*.

At least in part, the satire mocks the life-style that substitutes verbal riches for tangible comfort. Sheyne Sheyndl's descriptions of blood-spitting, sickly children, social ostracism, and vicious poverty, emphasize the full price each family paid for a schlemiel as breadwinner. Yet on the deepest level, Sholom Aleichem is making poverty the metaphor for spiritual wealth, and using the superabundance of language, particularly the rich veins of wit and humor, to suggest the cultural affluence that may be nourished by physical deprivation. The schlemiel is the bearer of this ironic meaning.

The conclusion of *Menahem Mendl* is an epitome of inversions, the quintessence of irony. The schlemiel-hero becomes an agent for life insurance, "the kind of business in which the more people die, the better it is for both the dead and the living." As Menahem Mendl explains it, the insurance business makes of death itself a blessing—not, heaven forbid, because of rewards in the life to come, but right here and now—by permitting a man to *make a living* out of death. One can clearly detect that by this point the author was finding it difficult to sustain the buoyant note of earlier episodes, and the subject of death is dominant and pervasive. Not only is dying the basis of the hero's occupation, it is the immediate cause of his adventure, since he alights from the train in a particular Bessarabian town in order to say Kaddish on the anniversary of his father's death. As usual, Menahem Mendl is taken in by swindlers, true connoisseurs of innocence, and he considers himself fortunate when he has escaped with his life. But this time, as if the saying of Kaddish were an intimation of his mortality, we follow him to no further adventures. In a postscript to his final letter, he announces his intention of going to America, ever optimistic of making his fortune, and bringing his family to join him.

From this concluding episode we perceive that even from the ultimate victimizer of innocents, Death, some slim pickings can be won by the human being scrambling for life. The automatic response of the schlemiel-hero, pushed into a confrontation with mortality, is given philosophic expression in the daily phrases of Jewish liturgy:

> The dead do not praise God, nor those who go down to silence.
> But we shall bless God, henceforth and forever, Hallelujah.

In his book *Tevye and Menahem Mendl as Expressions of Eternal Jewish Fate*,[12] I. I. Trunk distinguishes between these two major heroes: Menahem Mendl, he says, is pure instinct. Unlike Tevye the Dairyman, he does not experience ironic resignation, or ironic faith: he "expresses the elemental life instinct which does not see its tragic perspectives." But taken together, Menahem Mendl and his wife, Sheyne Sheyndl, do create the ironic juxtaposition that Tevye expresses in his own person, allowing the reader to weigh the fierce optimism against a tragic perspective. Together they represent the two extremes of faith and failure —she, material hopelessness; he, "the faith which is not grounded in any reality."

Menahem Mendl might be called the purest of Sholom

12. I. I. Trunk, *Tevye un Menakhem Mendl in yidishn velt goyrl* (New York, 1944), p. 30.

Aleichem's schlemiel studies because of his entirely limited self-awareness and his total insensitivity to the incongruities of his situation. Almost all his letters begin with the formal, letter-manual formula, followed immediately by a personal outburst of anguish:

> First of all, I'd like to inform you that, God be praised, I'm well and am enjoying life and peace. And may blessed God arrange matters so that we should always hear from one another only good news and glad tidings. Amen!
>
> Secondly, you should know that all week long I've been lying sick in Boiberik, that is, not dangerously sick, God forbid,—just suffering from a nasty illness. What happened is that I fell on my back, so that I'm now unable to turn from one side to the other.

This reads like a deposition in proof of Bergson's contention that "the basis of humor is rigidity, clashing with the inner suppleness of life . . . something mechanical encrusted upon the living." Menahem Mendl's failure to recognize the discrepancy between "firstly" and "secondly," and his mechanical adherence to form even when it bears no relation to actuality, provokes our laughter. But the religious phrasing of the dry formula, comic as it is, implies more than an ignorant rigidity; it comes to symbolize the simultaneous presence of two contradictory kinds of experience—the inherited, and unquestioning knowledge of God, and the daily experience of misery and frustration. Menahem Mendl is humorous because he is so consistently blind to these contradictions. At the same time Sholom Aleichem wants us to recognize that this very blindness rules out metaphysical doubt or despair. The "rigidity" that makes Menahem Mendl comical also keeps him throbbingly alive.

Menahem Mendl is a naked attempt to go beyond satire and to draw from an example of the most pitiable, laughable creature of society a model for psychic survival.

4. HOLOCAUST SURVIVOR

There is a tendency in modern Jewish scholarship to locate all sources of contemporary Jewish culture in the Bible. The term *schlemiel* has been dignified with this most kosher of etymological origins, and the same has been attempted for Jewish humor. One writer finds the paradigm of Biblical irony in laughter at idolatry, particularly Elijah's mockery of the priests of Baal. When the sacrifice of the priests remains on the altar, Elijah

mocked them, and said: "Cry aloud; for he is a god; either he is musing, or he is gone aside (attending to a call of nature) or he is on a journey, or peradventure he sleepeth, and must be awaked." (I Kings 18:27)

Commenting on this passage, Israel Knox writes that "the distinctive quality of Jewish humor is the will to righteousness,"[1] a quality that unites this early ironic outburst with much later ones, like that of the Maggid of Kosenitz who pleaded with God: "If you do not want to redeem your people Israel, then at least redeem the gentiles." According to the author, Jewish humor, including both examples, is

1. Israel Knox, "The Traditional Roots of Jewish Humor," *Judaism*, 12, no. 3 (Summer 1963): 327–37. The quotation is from page 333.

rooted in tragic optimism which grows from the simultaneous perception of two contradictory realities—"that the world is moving toward Messianic fulfillment, and that the future comes one day at a time."

The thesis, though interesting, concentrates on establishing precedent and similarities to the neglect of essential differences. Elijah, intent on righteousness, wants to laugh idolatry off the stage of history, and he mocks the priests because of his felt conviction that it can be done. His outburst is associated with one of the most convincing—because primitive—proofs of God's active presence to be found in the Scriptures, and the taunting, heavy irony heralds the strength of his triumph.

The concept of election is the source of both statements, but the Maggid's relation to the gentiles is tempered by knowledge of God's *inactivity*, and by the continuing superiority and domination of the nonelect. Elijah's religious conviction is reinforced by his experience; since the Maggid's equally strong conviction is not, his mockery must be directed largely toward himself. Modern Jewish humor grows from the tension of having to reconcile a belief as absolute as Elijah's with an experience of failure as absolute as that of the priests of Baal.

The schlemiel embodies this tension, being the equivalent of the defeated people, incapable of despair. In his prayer the Maggid is also playing the fool, because redemption of the gentiles, with a consequent end to the persecution of the Jews, would signify Jewish redemption, certainly in this world. His will to righteousness, when challenged by the obvious failure of righteousness, protected itself by ironying out the situation, thereby preserving the faith while allowing itself an outlet of aggression.

But in the contemporary phase of our subject, the question arises: at what point will failure break the back of faith? The destruction of European Jewry during World War II, the systematic slaughter of millions of people and the annihilation of thousands of communities has necessarily influenced our attitude towards the schlemiel as the victor in defeat. How does one retain the notion of psychic survival when its cost has been physical extinction? As long as the Jews were suffering from the old ills of hunger and humiliation and as long as pogroms were sporadic, the notion of a "triumph of identity despite failure of circumstance" could still carry some conviction. But after the entire populations of Kasrilevke and Tuneyadevke have been reduced to the ash of crematoria, does it not become a cruel sentimentality to indulge in schlemiel humor and to sustain a faith in the ironic mode?

And yet, strangely enough, the schlemiel has survived even the holocaust. Although almost too painful a subject for Yiddish fiction, which since the war has struggled through chronicles and lamentations with understandably little inclination for humor, he has found a home in American fiction and popular culture. The transplantation of this figure from Europe to America could be symbolized by the story "Gimpel the Fool," written by the Yiddish master, Isaac Bashevis Singer, and translated into English in 1953 by the American novelist Saul Bellow.[2]

"Gimpel Tam," a rare example of the schlemiel figure in postwar Yiddish fiction, is more correctly if less adequately translated as simpleton. The protagonist as his own narrator describes his youth and manhood in the shtetl of Frampol:

2. Isaac Bashevis Singer, "Gimpel the Fool," trans. Saul Bellow, in *Selected Short Stories of Isaac Bashevis Singer*, ed. Irving Howe (New York, 1966). First appeared in *Partisan Review*, May–June, 1953. All quotations are from this translation.

I am Gimpel the fool. I don't think myself a fool. On the contrary. But that's what folks call me. They gave me the name while I was still in school. I had seven names in all: imbecile, donkey, flax-head, dope, glump, ninny and fool. The last name stuck. What did my foolishness consist of? I was easy to take in . . .

He equates his foolishness with gullibility, the inclination to believe and trust in all that he is told. So he is married off to the town whore who is passed off as a virgin; accepts her explanation that the birth of their first-born son seventeen weeks after the wedding is the result of a familial genetic quirk; "fathers" six children not one of whom, as he later learns, is really his own; and foregoes the one real temptation to revenge himself against his mockers. The struggle between faith and skepticism is much more explicit in Gimpel than in any of his schlemiel-predecessors, a reflection of the much grimmer historical period within which he was created. As the opening sentences indicate, Gimpel is fully conscious of the distinction between the figure he cuts in the world and his own self-conception. Isaac Bashevis Singer has introduced the fool in Shakespearean ambiguity, a character who may be choosing to play the fool in order to retain his moral sanity in the face of universal cynicism.

As the story progresses, Gimpel's decision to remain gullible becomes ever more deliberate. Coming home unexpectedly one night and finding a stranger asleep with his wife, Gimpel realizes that "another in my place would have made an uproar," but he refrains from doing so lest he awaken the sleeping child: "A little thing like that—why frighten a little swallow?"

Later he resolves always to believe what he is told, in spite of the mockery and humiliation to which this credulity exposes him: "What's the good of *not* believing? Today it's your wife you don't believe in; tomorrow it's God Himself you won't take stock in."

The association of trust in one's unfaithful wife with trust in a God—also possibly unfaithful—widens the philosophic implications of Gimpel's struggle and indicates that Singer is probing a metaphysical and not merely a psychological condition. There is, throughout the narrative, deliberate ambiguity about what is alternately referred to as Gimpel's "faith" or "gullibility." Sometimes it's the result of having been genuinely duped; once he plays dumb to prevent innocent suffering; another time he chooses a life with love and without dignity to a life with dignity and without love. Finally, as the story nears its conclusion, Gimpel undergoes a moral crisis. When Elka, his wife, dies, admitting her deceptions, Gimpel is bereft of both dignity and love, and it is then that his soul goes up for grabs:

> One night, when the period of mourning was done, as I lay dreaming on the flour sacks, there came the Spirit of Evil himself and said to me, "Gimpel, why do you sleep?"
>
> I said, "What should I be doing? Eating *kreplach*?"
>
> "The whole world deceives you," he said, "and you ought to deceive the world in your turn."
>
> "How can I deceive all the world?" I asked him.
>
> He answered, "You might accumulate a bucket of urine every day and at night pour it into the dough. Let the sages of Frampol eat filth."
>
> "What about the judgment in the world to come?" I said.
>
> "There is no world to come," he said. "They've sold you a bill of goods and talked you into believing you carried a cat in your belly. What nonsense!"
>
> "Well then," I said, "and is there a God?"
>
> He answered, "There is no God either."
>
> "What," I said, "*is* there, then?"
>
> "A thick mire."

Gimpel is tempted to do the devil's bidding, but upon his wife's intervention, in a dream, he repents. Her face black from hellfire, she chides him for losing faith so easily. "Because I was false, is everything false too?" Is faith contingent upon human proofs? Gimpel's soul, whose essential quality is the ability to believe, would indeed have been lost had he satisfied himself with a mean revenge. He withstands the cheap psychological victory offered by the devil's vengeance, and sets out into the world voicing a formulated philosophy:

the longer I lived the more I understood that there were really no lies. Whatever doesn't really happen is dreamed at night. . . . No doubt the world is entirely an imaginary world, but it is only once removed from the true world. At the door of the hotel where I lie, there stands the plank on which the dead are taken away. The gravedigger Jew has his spade ready. The grave waits and the worms are hungry. . . . When the time comes I will go joyfully. Whatever may be there, it will be real, without complication, without ridicule, without deception. God be praised: there even Gimpel cannot be deceived.

Despite the obvious ironies of the story, the ending is "straight," or at least we are certain that Gimpel is not speaking ironically. In order to preserve his belief he has already sacrificed virility, pride, reputation, and the sweetness of revenge. He now calls the reality of the entire universe into question, preferring faith in the afterlife to cynicism in this one. We may compare this ending with a familiar Jewish joke about pious old Shloime's deathbed address to his children: "my whole life I endeavored to behave according to the Law and deprived myself of most pleasures, and lived a poor and miserable existence. I was always hoping that I would be rewarded in the beyond. I would laugh if there were nothing in the beyond."[3]

Both story and joke revolve on the final uncertainty. In Shloime's case we suspect—as he does—that his misery

3. The joke is cited in Reik, *Jewish Wit*, p. 65.

may have been in vain. But in Gimpel's case we believe—because he does—that his misery was surely not.

Reading "Gimpel the Fool" our rational prejudice is confronted with an appeal to a deeper truth, deeper because it frees a man from despair, permits him to live in harmony with his conscience, to practice goodness, and hope for justice.

Between opening and conclusion, the tone of the story changes noticeably as the character evolves from simpleton to saintly storyteller. The broad humor of the first three sections is saved from coarseness only by the delicacy of the irony. Its situations are the stuff of bedroom farces, but since the husband is amusing us at his own expense, there is compassion in our laughter. The conclusion, by contrast, is sober. A contemplative monologue supplants the lively narrative. The schlemiel youth grows into a mystical wanderer in a process that illuminates the connection between the two. In his simplicity the schlemiel ignores those same pragmatic social concerns which the mystic actively rejects through contemplation. The schlemiel's naïve substitution of his illusory world for the real one resembles the mystic's supernaturalism, a perhaps accidental resemblance that is shaped by Singer into an organic relation. In "Gimpel the Fool" the schlemiel-figure is explicitly raised to a higher level of significance by the association of a personality pattern with a metaphysic.

The antirational motif, which permeates Singer's work,[4]

4. See stories like "Esther Kreindel the Second," "A Wedding in Brownsville," "Yachid and Yachida," etc., whose literary point seems to be the inversion or obfuscation of normal divisions between what is real and what is not. In his less polished feuilletons which appear under the name of Itskhak Varshavski several times a week in the Yiddish daily, the New York *Forverts*, Singer frequently includes examples of ESP and other magical experiences that his readers have presumably brought to his attention.

exerts an obvious influence on his style. In the Gimpel story, and elsewhere, he uses the persona of a naïve storyteller as a convenient means of blurring the distinctions between appearance and more respectable forms of belief. Singer has emphasized that he is committed to the philosophy of "As if":

The "as if" is so much a part of our life that it really isn't artificial. ... Every man assumes he will go on living. He behaves *as if* he will never die.[5]

The "as if" lies at the heart of Gimpel's philosophy, and less self-consciously articulated, it is every schlemiel's method of coping with reality. Raised by Singer to his most exalted extreme, the schlemiel defies all rational distinctions and even the limits of life in his determination to remain fully human. The mystic's supernaturalism reflects his quest for God; but Gimpel's appeal to a transcendental standard is merely the result of having sought to live harmlessly among men.

Though man's heretofore unsuspected genius for evil has made the schlemiel-pose untenable, the story "Gimpel the Fool" suggests that even in the postwar period, authors may still turn to it in reaction to the alternative of toughness and pragmatism. In nonhumorous fiction of this type, the schlemiel is called a saint. André Schwartz-Bart's holocaust novel, *Le dernier des justes*,[6] introduces as hero a "lamed vovnik," one of the mythical thirty-six righteous men in whose grace the world continues to exist. The lamed vovnik, like Gimpel, remains true to human ideals by consciously denying the tyranny of reality. Before Ernie Levy dies in

5. Joel Blocker and Richard Elman, "An Interview with Isaac Bashevis Singer," *Commentary* 36, no. 5 (November 1963) : 365.
6. André Schwartz-Bart, *Le dernier des justes* (Paris, 1959). The quotation is from page 337.

Auschwitz, he shepherds a group of orphaned children to the gas chambers telling them of the kingdom of heaven where there is eternal joy, plenty to eat, and warmth unending. To an angry and cynical nurse who protests against these vicious lies (and even here male is believer, female is skeptic) Ernie says, "Madam, il n'y a pas de place ici pour la vérité." He too determines to live "as if" in order to lessen suffering, and because there is simply no place for reality, for truth, in a cattle car on its way to Auschwitz.

The schlemiel in humorous fiction, the saint in rhetoric heightened towards tragedy, reflect the actual response of almost an entire culture. Throughout the process of annihilation, the majority of Jews refused or were unable to face reality. The hymn of the concentration camps was the Ani Maamin: "I believe with perfect faith in the coming of the Messiah. And even though he is slow in coming (he is taking his own sweet time) yet even so, I believe." The song is ambivalent, like the Yiddish proverbs, but desperation has made the faith more fervent. In Arthur Koestler's wartime novel, *Arrival and Departure*, there is an account of another "hymn": as the "useless Jews" of a "mixed transport" are forced out of the cattle cars into the vans where they will be gassed, they sing the riddle folk song, "How shall we feast when Messiah arrives?" Those still waiting in the cattle cars supply the answers: "On Behemoth's meat shall we feast; wine from Mount Carmel shall we drink; Moses our Rabbi shall read Law for us; . . . and we shall make merry when Messiah arrives."[7] European Jews, whether we consider them saints or schlemiels, tended to resort to the same techniques of denial and avoidance, sublimation and rationalization, that the culture had so success-

7. Arthur Koestler, *Arrival and Departure* (London, 1943), chap. 3, part 7.

fully developed through many centuries. And in this wilful dream they were destroyed.[8]

A study of the schlemiel must take the real implications into account; for the character may, in his innocence, ignore the ultimate implications of his stance, but the modern reader will hardly be able to do so. Knowing what happened to Gimpel in the present century, the modern reader will be suspicious of passive responses, and the consolations of irony or faith.

If historical events have made us wary of the schlemiel-position, psychoanalysis has also put us on guard. The schlemiel, after all, is reconciled to the cardinal sin of

---

8. Cf. "People do not easily accept the fact that they are going to be killed; if they have the know-how to resist, they will defend themselves as best they can. If, on the other hand, they have unlearned the art of resistance, they will repress their knowledge of the true situation and will attempt to go on as though life could not change. The Jews could not resist. In complying with German orders they therefore tried, to the utmost of their ability, to ignore all evidence of danger and to forget all intimation of death. They pretended that nothing unusual was happening to them, and that belief became so crucial that they did anything to perpetuate it." Raul Hilberg, *The Destruction of the European Jews* (Chicago, 1961), p. 667 ff.

The "pretense" is usually interpreted with much greater sympathy, and with deeper understanding of its historical and psychological roots, in creative literature. See, e.g., Tadeusz Borowski, "The Man with the Package," *This Way for the Gas, Ladies and Gentlemen* (New York, 1968), pp. 127–31; The first part of Elie Wiesel's *Night* (New York, 1960); or this paragraph from Primo Levi's *Survival in Auschwitz* (*If This Be a Man*) (New York, 1959), describing the eve of departure for the death camp: "All took leave from life in the manner which most suited them. Some praying, some deliberately drunk, others lustfully intoxicated for the last time. But the mothers stayed up to prepare the food for the journey with tender care, and washed their children and packed the luggage; and at dawn the barbed wire was full of children's washing hung out in the wind to dry. Nor did they forget the diapers, the toys, the cushions and the hundred other small things which mothers remember and which children always need. Would you not do the same? If you and your child were going to be killed tomorrow, would you not give him to eat today?"

psychoanalysis, namely, failure. "Psychoanalysis," writes
Theodor Reik, "would characterize the schlemihl as a
masochistic character who has strong unconscious will to
fail and spoil his chances."[9] Explaining the popularity of
the schlemiel pose in modern culture, Albert Goldman calls
it an excuse, an apology, and a rationalization. "To be a
shlemihl is to have a stronghold for retreat."[10] Students, in
my experiences with the Gimpel story, tend to attack the
protagonist, saying, "He's just rationalizing because he
can't make it."

Yet the judgments of literature may be different from
those of history or even science. The psychoanalyst treats
the schlemiel concept as a neurotic symptom and tries to
determine the causes of a patient's failure in actual situations. The author may or may not be aware of the "masochistic need to fail" that dominates the subconscious of his
character, but such knowledge may be irrelevant to the
story. We may not willingly suffer fools in real life, yet in
our encounters among the pages of books we may learn from
them a wisdom more profound than our own. The irony of
"Gimpel the Fool" rests on our ability to perceive his failure as success. It is a philosophic equation that calls into
question our normal definitions of these antonymous terms.
Gimpel's antipragmatic philosophy mocks the need for
classification and rational explanation of which the tendency to define Gimpel as a masochist is itself a good example. A discussion of Gimpel as a failure, the historical
or psychoanalytic verdict, is from a literary standpoint
merely a way of avoiding the story. Even if in our personal

9. *Jewish Wit*, p. 41.

10. Albert Goldman, "Boy-man, Shlemihl: The Jewish Element in
American Humor," in *Explorations*, ed. Murray Mindlin and Chaim
Bermant (London, 1967), p. 14.

lives we subscribe to the moral code of a Beowulf, we should be able—as readers—to appreciate the challenge of the unheroic.

Mendele Mocher Sforim's traveller, Benjamin III, evolved from an object of ridicule into an ironic subject when he stepped into an environment more ridiculous and certainly more sinister than the one that had produced him. Because Sholom Aleichem seemed to accept the destructive environment as a given fact, he rendered what a critic has aptly called, "a judgment of love through the medium of irony."[11] Recreating the familiar schlemiel-figure in the aftermath of the holocaust, Singer made him a character of semifantastic fiction. Since the schlemiel is above all a re-action against the evil surrounding him, he must reject more and more as the evil increases; Gimpel is prepared to walk into eternity in pursuit of personal goodness.

11. Irving Howe, *A World More Attractive: A View of Modern Literature and Politics* (New York, 1963), p. 209.

5. THE AMERICAN DREAMER

When we first look for parallels, no atmosphere seems more unlike the repressive, poverty-ridden East European Jewish town than the open American society of mid-twentieth century. From 1881 onward, masses of Jewish immigrants fleeing pogroms and hunger came to what they called "The Golden Land," and despite hardships far greater than they had anticipated, their children did indeed grow up to opportunities the parents had once associated with a Messianic age. Yet, somehow, the policies of tolerance and the slow, steady climb into the middle, even upper-middle class, have not prevented Jews in America, including those of the third generation, from sharing many of the insecurities of their European forefathers. As experience soon showed, greater freedom encouraged a geographic and economic mobility which necessarily weakened communal and family cohesion. Not having to worry about annihilation, the community was threatened by corrosion from within, called variously acculturation, accommodation, or assimilation. The break-up of traditional Jewishness was occurring in Europe also, but there the older generation still stood on familiar ground, whereas in America all were newcomers, with the older immigrants far less sure footed than their adaptable young.

In spite of incomparably greater freedom, Jews were not absolved of their century-old culpability for the problems of Western civilization merely by the American Constitution. Subtle forms of discrimination / persisted, and widespread outbreaks of anti-Semitism continued to recur during critical periods. All this, added to the incalculable psychological aftereffects of the destruction of one-third of their coreligionists by the Nazis, helps to explain why American Jews do not sit as comfortably as statistical surveys of their creature comforts suggest they should.

The ambiguities of the Jews' position are manifested in the continuing vitality of Jewish humor, most of it structurally and thematically similar to its European source, though shorn of playful allusions and linguistic resonance. American Jewish folk humor, despite its vulgar exploitation by some professional entertainers, remains similar to Yiddish humor, and when English could not reproduce the ironic inflections and nuances of the Jewish joke, English was reshaped, grammatically and phonetically, in the Yiddish mold.[1] The schlemiel-figure, one of the basic characters in the Yiddish repertoire of humor, has continued in America to play his dual role as comic relief (thank God I'm not as simple as he is) and anxious reminder (there's something painfully familiar about that fellow).

There were the borscht-circuit routines of a comedian like Mikhl Rosenberg: when Getsl attended a baseball game, believing Yankl Stedium to be a new cantor, the audience laughed at a greenie even greener than itself, at its own pitiable attempt to embrace a new culture, and at the new

1. Unfortunately, the subject has been treated in a kitschy and imprecise manner: see, for example, Leo Rosten, *The Joys of Yiddish* (New York, 1968); Wallace Markfield, "The Yiddishization of American Humor," *Esquire*, October 1965, pp. 114–15. H. L. Mencken's analysis in *The American Language* (New York, 1937), p. 633–34, is interesting, but limited and outdated.

culture whose games were essentially so frivolous. The immigrant-as-schlemiel, obviously an outgrowth of Yiddish humor, continued the habit of challenging the environment in the very process of being baffled by it. So, for example, Leo Rosten's sentimental *Education of H*Y*M*A*N K*A*P*L*A*N* wins its heartiest laughs from the broken English of the adult student: "Ve got Memorable Day, Fort July, . . . and for de feenish from Voild Var—Armistress Day."[2] But the real foil of the book is the pedantic WASP instructor, Mr. Parkhill. The title of the book refers not only to what Hyman Kaplan learns, but to the warmth and unembarrassed heartiness he teaches.

While the hapless immigrant, his situation no less precarious than before, may be an organic outgrowth of European Jewish humor, the tenacious hold of the schlemiel on the American Jewish consciousness can be better demonstrated by reference to the humor of a much later and quite dissimilar situation, the Arab-Israeli Six-Day War of June 1967. The State of Israel is acknowledged as the birthplace of "a new Jew." Certainly during that war, if not before, the cliché of a bronzed warrior emerged ready to replace the older cliché of a wizened rabbi. Yet in the bookstores of New York, alongside chest-thumping accounts of victory were items like *Irving of Arabia: An unorthodox interpretation of the Israeli-Arab War* which shows a soldier going off to battle with his mother in the background, pleading, "Marvin, please. Take your galoshes"; or the poster of a shrunken Hasid emerging from a telephone booth in a familiar cape bearing the inscription "Super-Jew." A portion of the American Jewish public, perhaps as an instinctive reflex of self-protection, continued to trace the old

2. Leo Calvin Rosten, *The Education of H*Y*M*A*N K*A*P*-L*A*N* (New York, 1937), p. 74.

outlines under the new events. Better to stick to the identification with the schlemiel-loser than to risk believing in a newfound strength. Or perhaps from where he sits, the American Jewish humorist perceives the continuing vulnerability of the Jewish position, for all its seeming might. Whether through fear or perspicacity, the cartoonists provided a war as it would have been fought (or not) by American Jews, juxtaposing the success theme of Israel with the submission and adaptation themes of Europe. The humor of cartoons like that of a soldier being sewn together out of material scraps, each donated by the Segals or Cohens or Goldbergs in loving honor of the Crespis, the Feldmans, or Levys, derives from the recognition that whatever the Israeli has achieved, the American Jew remains the compromiser. His business is not war, but *shmates*. Perhaps the Israeli's proficiency in warfare has only reinforced the American Jew's contrasting perception of himself as schlemiel.

The Jewish fool made the transition from Europe to America at the level of popular culture and did not flourish in serious American Jewish fiction until the postwar period. At the earlier stages of acculturation, this literature dealt with social problems so dramatic that characters were subsumed under their social units of profession, class, or generation: the radical, dedicated labor leader; second-generation crusading lawyer; pugnacious purveyor of entertainment; penurious chess-playing philosopher.[3] The Jew was engaging America, whether for good or otherwise, and Jewish writers refereeing the encounter portrayed it

3. A more exact breakdown of Jewish character types in the literature and drama of the 1920s and 1930s in Joseph Mersand, *Traditions in American Literature: A Study of Jewish Characters and Authors* (New York, 1939).

along lines of sociological differentiation. It was during World War II, when younger writers took their birthright —now American—for granted, and when the social drama, in its limited variations, had been worn to a cliché, that novels began to explore the character of Jewish characters. In this new typology based on psychological distinctions, the schlemiel became almost as popular as mamma.

Natural as his emergence within Jewish culture may have been, the loser-as-winner was not an indigenous American folk-type, and there is much in his makeup that still seems to go against the American grain. Studies of traditional American folk humor portray quite different comic heroes of a decidedly practical bent, resourceful and hard-headed pragmatists who inevitably outwit the fools, be they dimwits or woolly intellectuals. Pioneers and neopioneers admired the reality-rootedness of Poor Richards, Davy Crocketts, and down-to-earth frontiersmen who made "gumption into a national religion."[4]

Nothing nicer could be said of a man that "He's got horse sense"; no one was a better comic target than the enthusiast.

Schlemiel humor, which makes hardship into laughter through recourse to the irrational and absurd, would have been as unpalatable to earlier generations of Americans as gefilte fish, a similar device for camouflaging rotten leavings as a delicacy.

The more recent hospitable reception of the Yiddish strain into American humor cannot be explained merely by reference to the influx of Jews into American society or to

4. Walter Blair, *Horse Sense in American Humor* (Chicago, 1942); Constance Rourke, *American Humor: A Study of the National Character* (New York, 1931).

the humanization of minority group caricatures.[5] When America as a whole began to experience itself as a "loser" after World War II and ever more insistently in the 1950s, the schlemiel was lifted from his parochial setting into national prominence. Though the romantic search for a classic hero was slow to die—the authors were themselves the Gatsbys—the antiheroic mode inevitably gained, admitting to the limitation of human frontiers, even in America. The more America felt its age and the shrinking opportunities for renewal or even improvement, the more the Jewish ghetto experience could provide the model for a new sensibility. But the admission of a specifically Jewish humor was only gradual, and the initial reception of the schlemiel was frosty.

One of the most popular and acclaimed books of the 1920s was *The Sun Also Rises*.[6] At the acknowledged risk of setting up a straw man, we could examine the icy beginnings of the schlemiel in American fiction by referring to its antagonist, the Jew, Robert Cohn. Hemingway poetically and with precision intertwined the two thematic lines of the novel, each introduced by its caption: "You are all a lost generation," the verdict of Gertrude Stein; and "One generation passeth away, and another generation cometh; but the earth abideth forever," the lofty, impersonal judgment of Ecclesiastes. Sympathetically, Hemingway portrays the impotent members of the lost generation, unable to overcome the physical and psychological wounds sustained in the war. They may move, the book suggests, beyond self-pity to the manly grace of the quoted passage from Ecclesiastes

5. Constance Rourke makes this prediction in the conclusion of her book.

6. Ernest Hemingway, *The Sun Also Rises* (New York, 1926).

if they learn restraint and self-control. As has often been noted, the aesthetic and moral core of the novel can be located in Romero's capework and in his ability to hold "his purity of line through the maximum of exposure." Of this code Robert Cohn is the foil.

Cohn betrays all the book's standards, especially the aesthetic. There is in his life-style no containment, no purity, not even any line. When he drinks a lot, Cohn gets drunk and sick. When he falls in love, he is as shameless as Swann, the hopeless victim of his emotion. He is, in Mark Spilka's phrase, "The last chivalric hero," but in a book built on the premise that love is dead, any man who surrenders himself to it is a fool, or at least "a case of arrested development." Where restraint equals manhood, emotional self-indulgence must be puerile, and Cohn in his Princeton jersey remains the eternal adolescent. The verdict on him is thumbs down all around. "I hate him," says Jake. "I hate him too," says Brett. "I hate his damned suffering."

Phenomenologically, Cohn is almost a classic schlemiel. We recognize in his impressionable reading of W. H. Hudson exactly the same escapist, dreaming qualities that made Benjamin III such a devoted reader of "bobe mayses" and Don Quixote a victim of romances. He is the same patsy for overbearing women, bullied by Frances who wants him, and by Brett who doesn't. He accepts humiliation; he is accused of reveling in it. He is a tactless blunderer, seemingly unconscious of the derision he inspires in Harvey, Mike, Bill, the chorus.

But Cohn remains a schlemiel-manqué, because the book realizes neither the humor of his condition nor any irony in his failure as compared with the "success" of the in-group. Romero the Bullfighter is still the traditional Western hero in this work, a man of dignity, truth-to-self, physical courage, romantic polish, masculine beauty, the old-fashioned virtues. His portrait affirms the possibilities of heroism in the traditional sense of the word, the possibilities of success and of tragedy. The protagonists, Jake and Brett, are incapable of achieving his sublimity, but they at least recognize the higher standards he embodies, whereas Cohn, who "had a chance to behave so well," behaves shamefully and shows no understanding of manhood or manners. He is, among tough guys, a sniveler. Hemingway writes about the schlemiel from the standpoint of the gentile Westerner, and concludes that his qualities are wholly defeatist and distasteful.

The widespread anti-Semitism among American writers in the early decades of this century derived in part from their apprehension that something was corrupting the American Adam and corroding American ideals, that "something" being associated with the Jew. Cohn's is the most thorough portrayal of the menace (and for this reason the least offensive), although for mythical intensity Fitzgerald's Wolfsheim, the man who undermined American morals by fixing the World Series, takes the prize. In addition to the usual reasons for, and expressions of, hostility toward Jews, the arrival of large masses of Eastern European Jewish immigrants to America coincided with rapid urbanization and the end of political isolationism, with the dying away of an older way of life. Some observers saw a relation of cause and effect between these two sets of events. Henry Adams writes in distress from Washington in 1914:

The atmosphere really has become a Jew atmosphere. It is curious and evidently good for some people, but it isolates me. I do not know the language, and my friends are as ignorant as I. We are still in power, after a fashion. Our sway over what we call society is undisputed. We keep Jews far away, and the anti-Jew feeling is

quite rabid. We are anti-everything and we are wild up-lifters; yet
we somehow seem to be more Jewish every day.[7]

Adams uses the word *Jewish* in the broadest sociological
sense, making a connection between the new "Jew atmosphere" and all that threatens "what we call society." Similarly, twelve years later, when Hemingway created a
Jewish character to stand in opposition to all he called
society, the two versions were not as disparate as we might
want to believe. The myth of American innocence was being
sullied, and what could explain it away better than the myth
of Jewish guilt? By negative implication Jews became the
symbols of encroaching commercialism, middlebrowism,
and emotionalism: "the Jew at the bottom of the pile."

The association of these changes in American life with
Jewishness seems to have remained (though the "culprit" is
obviously undeserving of the compliment), but the judgmental weight of the words "Jew atmosphere" was gradually inverted. Explaining the move of the Jewish writer
into the center of American culture, Leslie Fiedler is almost
bored by the obvious:

The background is familiar enough: the gradual breaking up of
the Anglo-Saxon domination of our imagination: the relentless
urbanization which makes rural myths and images no longer central
to our experience; the exhaustion as vital themes of the Midwest and
of the movement from the provinces to New York or Chicago or
Paris; the turning again from West to East from our own heart-
land back to Europe; and the discovery in the Jews of a people
essentially urban, essentially Europe-oriented, a ready-made image
for what the American longs to or fears he is being forced to become.[8]

7. Henry Adams, "From a Letter to Charles Milnes Gaskell," in *The
Jew in a Gentile World*, ed. Arnold Rogow (New York, 1961).
8. Leslie Fiedler, "Saul Bellows," in *Saul Bellow and the Critics*, ed.
Irving Malin (New York, 1967), pp. 2–3.

The accusation once leveled against the outsider has
become his password into the inner circle of belonging.
America is, after all, one of the oldest republics in the world.
If the Russian Jew was once insecure because of pogrom
threats and the arbitrary disfavor of government, metro-
politan Americans fear a nuclear pogrom and the arbitrary
disfavor of their gun-toting neighbors. Menahem Mendl,
the luftmensch, represented the insecurity of the middle-
man, then still a marginal economic type; nowadays the
majority of Americans are employed in services—selling
and waiting on tables; management, communication; per-
sonnel selection; decorator centers; marketing research and
analysis; message headquarters—similarly "living on air,"
only in a nattier suit. Moreover, Americans inherit a tradition of political messianism, the ideals of Jeffersonian
democracy. The tension of maintaining faith in the democratic process while living in a political slough of despond
is not at all unlike the ironic traditional tension of the Jew.
And if the Jew's experience resembles the normative American experience, then it stands to reason that the schlemiel,
who embodied so much of the irony of the Jewish situation,
can become the ironic vehicle on a national scale.

So it is hardly surprising that Saul Bellow, in one of those
unspectacular passages that can later be pointed to as a
turning point in cultural history, should have opened his
first novel, *Dangling Man,* by throwing down the gauntlet to
Hemingway:

There was a time when people were in the habit of addressing
themselves frequently and felt no shame at making a record of their
inward transactions. But to keep a journal nowadays is considered a
kind of self-indulgence, a weakness, and in poor taste. For this is an
era of hardboiled-dom. Today, the code of the athlete, of the
tough-boy—an American inheritance, I believe, from the English

gentleman—that curious mixture of striving, asceticism, and rigor, the origins of which some trace back to Alexander the Great—is stronger than ever. Do you have feelings? There are correct and incorrect ways of indicating them. Do you have an inner life? It is nobody's business but your own. Do you have emotions? Strangle them. To a degree, everyone obeys this code. And it does admit of a limited kind of candor, a closemouthed straightforwardness. But on the truest candor, it has an inhibitory effect. Most serious matters are closed to the hardboiled. They are unpracticed in introspection, and therefore badly equipped to deal with opponents whom they cannot shoot like big game or outdo in daring.[9]

Bellow consciously set out to write an American novel, centered on a hero whose purity of line through the maximum of exposure could only be the spreading circumference of a pot belly. The new spokesman for an altered America would be more like Cohn than like Jake Barnes, and the reader would presumably accept the author's assumption that Romeros were as outdated as Lord Fauntleroys.

The first mutation would be rhetoric. In place of the monosyllabic, uninflected style that Hemingway perfected, Bellow intended to talk, "and if I had as many mouths as Siva has arms and kept them going all the time I still could not do myself justice." The need for a new style arose from the quest for a new truth; because, as Bellow's fictional spokesman, Joseph, explains, on the *truest* candor the tight-lipped straightforwardness has an inhibitory effect. Hemingway's prose is stripped to the bone. There is no cant, there are no frills of sentimentality. No lies are told. But the absence of lies is not synonymous with truth. The intricacies of rich personality cannot be explored without recourse to the emotive and intellectual probing of sentiment and conscience that Hemingway so consistently avoided. In Hem-

9. Saul Bellow, *Dangling Man* (New York, 1944).

ingway's fiction nature's cues are reliable, whereas man's decisions and actions are disconcertingly arbitrary. Thus Nick, during his solitary trip up the "Big, Two-Hearted River," stays in harmony with nature by never imposing his human frailties on her perfection. When Nick is faced with the decidedly human task of making coffee, he recalls the varied, vying opinions of his companions on former trips, and finally making the coffee according to one of their recipes, he finds it too terrible to drink.

Bellow would agree that human behavior is erratic and irrational, but this, for him, is part of its charm. Human life is by definition more complex than animal life, and its complexity thus becomes an index of its humanity. As Joseph, the hero of *Dangling Man*, hangs suspended between choices of induction or independent isolation, the author introduces Joseph's "companion," a Talmudic dybbuk known as "The Spirit of Alternatives," or alternately, as "But on the Other Hand," or again, as "Tu As Raison Aussi." Like any authentic Talmudic debate, Joseph's dialogue with his superego, or projected antitype, is not mere pilpul—not dialectic athletics for its own sake—but rather a sharpened quest for what is right. The rhetorical style, the very sentence structure, suggests the ambiguities and intricacies of Joseph's mind. He says, "My talent, if I have one at all, is for being a citizen, or what is today called, most apologetically, a good man." The qualifying clausality of the syntax reflects the moral and psychological deflections on the way to the goal. The garrulous monologues of Joseph and other Bellow characters are filled with suggestions of compromise, uncertainty, weakness, and failure, the inevitable consequence of urban, democratic living.

Complexity is not the only index of the human condition in Bellow's first novel. To the same degree that Hemingway had emphasized the virtue of stoical containment, Bellow embraced the opposing value of committed emotional involvement. "Trouble," says Joseph, "like physical pain, makes us actively aware that we are living, and when there is little in the life we lead to hold and draw and stir us, we seek and cherish it, preferring embarrassment or pain to indifference."

This new emphasis on intensity as one of the basic components of the schlemiel-character in American fiction indicates his main point of departure from European sources. The simpleton of the earlier works was a symbol of unbroken faith against almost universal skepticism and against fierce physical persecution. The American Jewish author is not concerned with faith-rootedness—if anyone is—nor with the survival of a God-centered community. His schlemiel is not even remotely symbolic of a people. He is an expression of heart, of intense, passionate feeling, in surroundings that stamp out individuality and equate emotion with unreason. The schlemiel is used as a cultural reaction to the prevailing Anglo-Saxon model of restraint in action, thought, and speech. What is Bellow's metaphor of Siva moving its many mouths and arms if not the Semitic stereotype of vulgar volubility? The Yiddish schlemiel was an expression of faith in the face of material disproofs. The American schlemiel declares his humanity by loving and suffering in defiance of the forces of depersonalization and the ethic of enlightened stoicism.

Many of these figures are named with heart: There is Levin, of Malamud's novel, *A New Life*, called Lev, the Hebrew word for heart; *Herzog*, meaning heart, speak; *Miss Lonelyhearts*, Nathanael West's early forerunner of the schlemiel; Rosie Lieber, the speaker in Grace Paley's monologue "Goodbye and Good Luck"; Bellow's Clarence

Feiler of *The Gonzaga Manuscripts*. Writing on Malamud, a critic says, "The Jew has typically a 'heart condition' and this is perhaps Malamud's central metaphor."[10] This lovely formulation applies generally to the schlemiel as a character in American fiction.

In English, as in Yiddish literature, the monologue is a preferred form, so that the speaker's position may have the force to engage the reader's allegiance despite its feeble objective base. In English, as in Yiddish, the monologue may be used for humor, and when the speaker is "from the Yiddish," the inflected language is itself a source of fun.

Inflections, even in second generation characters like Alexander Portnoy, provide comic material and a clue to the social standing of the speaker. They may also release a potential in the language, since the immigrant, like the child, is unhampered by restrictions of grammar and may free hidden linguistic possibilities that remain confined in grammatical formality. Grace Paley's memorable "Goodbye and Good Luck" applies this technique in one of the few schlemiel stories whose leading character is a woman. Unburdening herself to Lillie, her niece, Aunt Rosie mocks the notion that she is pitiable:

If there was more life in my little sister [Lillie's mother] she would know my heart is a regular college of feelings and there is such information between my corset and me that her whole married life is a kindergarten. . . .

I am good-natured—you know fat people are like that—kind, and I thought to myself, poor Mama . . . she married who she didn't like, a sick man, his spirit already swallowed up by God. He never washed. He had an unhappy smell. His teeth fell out, his hair disappeared, he got smaller, shriveled up little by little till goodbye and good luck he was gone and only came to Mama's mind when

10. Gabriel Pearson, "Bernard Malamud and the Jewish Arrival," *Explorations*, ed. M. Mindlin and C. Bermant (London, 1967), p. 28.

she went to the mailbox under the stairs to get the electric bill. In
memory of him and out of respect to mankind, I decided to live
for love.[11]

Aunt Rosie recalls how she fell in love with Volodya Vlashkin, "called by the people of those days the Valentino of
Second Avenue"; how she left her mother for her lover,
although she knew he had "a wife, children, the whole
combination"; how she stayed true to him for years, "Oi,
Vlashkin, if you are my friend, what is time?" Only when
Vlashkin is divorced by his wife, who has grown tired of
having him around, does Rosie win a proposal from him.
As she recedes into the sunset, Aunt Rosie calls out her
farewell:

> My goodness, I am already late. Give me a kiss. After all, I
> watched you grow from a plain seed. So give me a couple wishes on
> my wedding day. A long and happy life. Many years of love. Hug
> Mama, tell her from Aunt Rose, goodbye and good luck.

Fat, romantic Rosie is played off against the flat, middle-
class values of her sister, obviously to her own advantage.
The energy of the monologue is the extension of her emotional nature which is her one and only asset. She loves
Volodya because of the emotions he is able to arouse in his
audiences, and she is satisfied with herself because by feeling, she too has lived. The story is soaked in irony, there
being some distance between the monologist's interpretation of her actions and the reader's independent judgment.
Yet Lillie, the silent witness, is with her Aunt, not her
mother, in more than the physical sense. Like Bloom, Aunt
Rosie wins the allegiance and interest of the child who is
not her own by offering more than the natural parent can.

11. Grace Paley, "Goodbye and Good Luck," in *The Little Disturbances of Man* (New York, 1959). The quotations are from pages 9
and 20.

Objectively, Rosie's life is such a failure that her mother and normally settled sister bemoan her pitiable fate. By her pathetic insistence on a life of virtue once her lover is free ("How could you ask me to go with you on trains to stay in strange hotels, among Americans, not your wife?"), she confirms that her values are in no way different from those of her family. Only her priorities are different, and these, in her own eyes, make Rosie the most fortunate "lieber" of all—fat, aging bride though she is. Actually, her romantic attachment is rewarded: albeit on the rebound, she does get her man.

When it is not direct or in diary, the monologue may take an epistolary form. Thus Isaac Rosenfeld's wartime story, "The Hand That Fed Me."[12] is in many respects similar to Saul Bellow's novel, a resemblance which is not surprising in the light of the friendship and shared interests of the two authors. Written as a series of five letters from Joseph Feigenbaum to a certain Ellen, between December 21 and December 31, the story studies intelligence in the service of fantasy. Joseph replies to a Christmas card he has received from Ellen, a girl he met in the WPA office three years earlier and with whom he spent that one and only day. Her unexpected card, followed by no further communication, triggers off a succession of fantasies, including an intricate analysis of the nonexistent relationship. Joseph constructs a romance—much as one constructs a philosophic system—which has no touchstones in reality, and which elicits no actual response. Because he is not unaware of the irony of his condition, Joseph, living as he says "in what I consider to be a state of exile," must resort to paradoxes. His self-deception is also a form of self-analysis; his loneliness

12. Isaac Rosenfeld, "The Hand That Fed Me," in *Modern Jewish Stories*, ed. Gerda Charles (Englewood Cliffs, N. J., 1963), pp. 225–43.

forces him to clutch at an aging memory, but in addressing
the memory, he creates a form of dialogue. The mounting
humiliation he feels after so thoroughly exposing his love to
rejection leads him beyond humiliation to belief in his own
potential happiness:

> I still believe in human happiness, and in my own to boot. If I can-
> not make my claim on you, I will make it on life, demand that
> existence satisfy the longings it arouses. It must, it must! For that is
> happiness: the conviction that something is necessary. . . .
> We are accustomed to sing the joys of the happy, the fulfilled men.
> Let us also sing the joys of the desolate, the empty men. Theirs is the
> necessity without fulfillment but it is possible that even to them—
> who knows?—some joy may come.

The very process of giving voice to his despair has made
Joseph aware, on the eve of a new year, of his willingness
to risk disappointment and, it must follow, of his belief in
joy.

> I am cushioned at the bottom and only look forward to what I may
> expect. For after all, what is humiliation? It does not endure for-
> ever. And when it has led us underground to our last comfort, look,
> it has served its purpose and it is gone. Who knows when new
> heights may not appear? A man has only so much in common with
> his experience. The rest he derives from God knows where.

Puffed up in this quasi-Biblical rhetoric, Joseph, a little
man, seems littler still. But as Joseph is not fully bound by
his experience, so too he surmounts his own irony, and the
clinical diagnosis of the protagonist is not the story's. Only
a sick man can conduct a fiery, ten-day correspondence with
a woman who has sent him a Christmas card after a one-day
meeting some three years earlier. On the other hand, no
mere neurotic could so accurately, in the process of laying
bare his sickness, uncover his commitment to health. The
analysand so clearly alive to the world around him and to

his own thwarted interaction with it is himself an analyst, and when in the final letter he pronounces himself cured, he is not unconvincing.

These inversions are made acceptable by the contrasting hollowness of everything around. The Josephs of Rosenfeld and Bellow both inhabit a war-depressed society, in which communism has been discredited as a moral alternative, and democratic human choices limited to military induction or the WPA. The emotional-intellectual odysseys of both heroes are schlemielish, since real heroes would have embarked on real, that is, actual quests. These men are literally and symbolically unemployed. Each of them, aware of his foolishness, is filled with self-mockery. Only against the unimaginative humdrum of surrounding life-styles does their own intensity present a welcome value. As faith was an alternative to failure, so intensity—expressed as rhetorical intensity—becomes an alternative to regimentation or plain dullness.

Stern, by Bruce Jay Friedman,[13] is not a monologue, and with the third-person form comes a deliberate increase of distance between the schlemiel's point of view and that of the novel. Stern suffers from an ulcer, the localized symbol of all his hurt, and actual cause of his anxiety and pain. The ulcer is a kind of "heart condition" in that it grows as Stern begins to feel his estrangement and to long for accepting love; but the diagnosis of pain in a lower, less poetic organ, is symptomatic of Friedman's harsher, lower form of humor. *Stern* is another study of the sick man as the relatively healthy man, the psychological equivalent of loser as winner, but one that exposes the full horror of this inversion.

Urbanite recently transposed to suburbia, Jew among

13. Bruce Jay Friedman, *Stern* (New York, 1962).

gentiles, the protagonist is introduced as the victim of a
symbolic cuckolding—the burly, mythical "goy" of the
neighborhood has knocked down and "seen" his wife. Stern,
who "had waited . . . for the day his wife would say this to
him," a victim even before the specific occasion defined
the nature of his ordeal, sets out to avenge the act. Instead
he tentatively punches himself in the belly, and the spreading sweetness of the ulcer pain makes its first appearance.

In his article "Boy-man, Shlemihl," Albert Goldman
calls *Stern* "the most vividly drawn, the most completely
unmasked schlemihl created by any modern American
writer."[14] If truth is more vivid because it is unpleasant,
then Goldman is right. Satire unmasks more than humor
does by stripping away more of the trappings of civilization
to concentrate on the naked ape beneath: to this extent Stern
is the most "unmasked" of modern schlemiels. In *Stern*,
Jewishness is just an irrational remnant of sterile forms
("In arguments with friends as to whose grandmother was
more religious Stern would weigh in with 'Mine *opens* the
damned synagogue' and he would generally walk off with
the honors"); family is a Mafia-type arrangement govern-
ing through overt or covert blackmail. Stern's magnanim-
ities are interpreted as compensatory acts, and the dynamics
of his little kindnesses are bared, as though in a glass clock
where all the working parts are shown in motion:

He was afraid of the boy's sudden eruption and wondered why the
boy couldn't be nice to him all the time. Violence was such a waste.
It didn't accomplish anything. . . . Stern wanted to tell the boy: "Be
nice to me at all times and I'll tell you things that will make you
smart. I'll lend you books and, when we both get out, take you to
a museum, explaining any hard thing."

14. Albert Goldman, "Boy-man, Schlemihl," p. 14.

The liberal's emphasis on civilization is only, as Callicles insisted, the outgrowth of his terror.

Friedman's humor is more reductionist than Bellow's or Rosenfeld's; that is to say, it is less humane. In works of complex irony, like Italo Svevo's *Confessions of Zeno*, the narrator offers several alternative explanations for his actions, contrasting his motives with others' interpretations of those motives, and with the unanticipated end results. The idea emerges of man as an intricate, irreducible being who is both funnier and more precious than he ordinarily appears. But the black humor of *Stern* explains away all motives, presenting a view of man that is necessarily meaner and more circumscribed. The final pages of the book show Stern's overflowing sympathy, which is *almost* recognized as the manifestation of a great soul. A year and a half after the initial provocation, he returns to fight the enemy, now with the requisite courage, but with an overly sensitive heart:

He saw [the man's] socks . . . faded blue anklets with little green clocks on them. They were cut low, almost disappearing into his slippers, and reminded Stern of those worn by an exchange student from Latvia at college who had brought along an entire bundle of similar ones. Now Stern felt deeply sorry for the man's powerful feet, which were always to be encased in terrible refugee anklets, and for a second he wanted to embrace them.

Stern's capacity to admit the humanity of his adversary, his vision of the enemy as just another "refugee," could have made him a moral hero. Instead he is cut down to size in the final paragraph where all this emotion is exposed for the theatrical extravagance the author finds it to be.

The book remains critical of the protagonist and uses the weapons of satire to deflate him. Nevertheless, even Stern's ineffectual sensitivity is healing. If at the end he is still not at home in the world, he is at least more at home in his home, as husband and father and man.

These four characters—Aunt Rosie, the two Josephs, and Stern—are examples of alienation and marginality, but like the prototypical schlemiel of Yiddish fiction, not entirely so. Each of them is rooted in the very familial or communal structure from which he is estranged, and that belonging, that entrenchment, is not merely historical, a piece of biographical data, but a vigorous and continuing part of his emotional life. In one way or another, Aunt Rosie, Joseph Feigenbaum, Stern, and of course Bellow's Joseph, *elect* induction to marriage, to love, to the army, to life. Each is maimed—ulcerous, fat, or neurotic—yet interpreted as an example of relative health. There is about each of them a touch of cheerfulness, unwarranted by the facts of the case, but there nonetheless.

The Yiddish schlemiel did not abandon faith in the Almighty simply because he was confronted by proofs of God's perfidy. He learned to live suspended between belief and skepticism, perfectly and eternally balanced. Just so, in a different anthropological climate, the American Jewish schlemiel does not withdraw from human society simply because he and it are doomed to defeat. He learns to live within a continuing tension between belief in man and radical frustration. At the basis of Yiddish humor is a century-old metaphysical dilemma. From this the American Jewish authors have extracted merely the psychological paradox: that the knowledge of life's futility, reinforced by daily experiences, does not invalidate an urgent insistence on joy, irrational as such emphasis may be. The insistence is foolish, since man, a Pavlovian subject, is expected to learn from experience and to modify his ambitions accordingly. He is supposed, returning for a moment to Hemingway's standards, to puncture false hopes of happiness with wise resignation: "Yes. . . . Isn't it pretty to think so?" The schlemiel is incapable or unwilling to make this move. So he continues to dream, or to fight for love, or to seek it, and according to the bias of his author is either ironically rewarded or satirically deflated for his efforts. Bellow's Herzog thrusts out his opening line in almost Whitmanic defiance: "If I am out of my mind, it's all right with me . . ."

6. THE SCHLEMIEL AS LIBERAL HUMANIST

Schlemiels abound in Bellow's fiction, even in the stories he chooses to translate and anthologize.[1] Bellow is concerned, throughout his literary development, with the diminished stature of the individual in everyone's perception but his own:

It's obvious to everyone that the stature of characters in modern novels is smaller than it once was, and this diminution powerfully concerns those who value existence. I do not believe that the human capacity to feel or do can really have dwindled or that the quality of humanity has degenerated. I rather think that people appear smaller because society has become so immense.[2]

The diminution of the hero is only a matter of perspective; the actual ratio of aspiration to human accomplishment has not appreciably altered.

Bellow's considerable achievement as a writer has been

1. Saul Bellow, ed., *Great Jewish Short Stories* (New York, 1963). The volume includes at least ten schlemiel tales, among them Grace Paley's "Goodbye and Good Luck," Isaac Bashevis Singer's "Gimpel the Fool" (in Bellow's translation), Philip Roth's "Epstein," Sholom Aleichem's "On Account of a Hat," and Bernard Malamud's "The Magic Barrel." Bellow is also the translator of Sholom Aleichem's "Eternal Life" in *A Treasury of Yiddish Stories*, ed. Howe and Greenberg (New York, 1953).

2. Stanley Kunitz, ed., *Twentieth Century Authors*, First Supplement (New York, 1955), p. 73.

to portray, against the unquestionably dwarfing forces of modern society, the honest, often successful struggle of the individual striving to define himself as a man within a narrowing range of active possibilities.

The most Jewish of Bellow's heroes, his most typical schlemiel, and most entertaining humorist, is Moses El-kanah Herzog, who is provided with a far more detailed personal history and more substantial biography than such characters usually receive, even in the author's other works. It is only when reading the evocative descriptions of Her-zog's childhood and the ample information on his profes-sional and personal life that we realize, by contrast, how poorly documented are the lives of our other characters and how thinly their roots have been sketched. Schlemiel portrayals that emphasize economic or social insecurity have no need for such sensuous background: in fact, the very thinness of personal history brings out in bolder relief the uncertainty of the character's position and destiny. But *Herzog*, which explores the psychology of the schlemiel, necessarily dips into childhood to explain the responses of the adult.

His father, Herzog candidly recalls, was an urbane Mena-hem Mendl:

> In 1913 he bought a piece of land near Valleyfield, Quebec, and failed as a farmer. Then he came into town and failed as a baker; failed in the dry-goods business; failed as a jobber; failed as a sack manufacturer in the War, when no one else failed. He failed as a junk dealer. Then he became a marriage broker and failed—too short-tempered and blunt. And now he was failing as a boot-legger, on the run from the Provincial Liquor Commission. Making a bit of a living.[3]

At the same time, this is the father, "a sacred being, a king."

3. Saul Bellow, *Herzog* (New York, 1964), p. 137. The other extended quotations are from pages 230, 104–5, 170, 238, 119–20, 86, and 77.

And as for Herzog's mother, she pampered and over-protected the children. The daughter must have piano lessons. Her precious Moses must grow up to be a great *lamden*—a rabbi. She pulled him on a sled, sacrificing her strength to her children. Moses, the Jewish immigrant child, "dear little Yingele," was the traditional repository of parental dreams. Center of the universe, he experienced, as he tells us, "a wider range of human feelings than he had ever again been able to find." The boy is the focus of love, but the failing father gives ominous warning of things that might lie ahead. Here, on the familial level, is the theological paradox, domesticated: the Jew as the repository of God's Torah, His hope, living in the temporal world as one of a persecuted, despised minority. The Jewish son, like Herzog, experiences the paradox in his own home. Elected to embody all the unfulfilled aspirations of his parents, he knows before he sets out that he will never achieve them: his father's presence tells him so. Yet, as in the national idea of election, the warmth and love given to the child communicate a sense of importance, an idea of worth and a framework of meaning that are never entirely eradicated in spite of all subsequent battering. Herzog writes his unfinished, unposted letters. He is nonetheless able to say: "*I* am Herzog. I have to *be* that man. There is no one else to do it."

The family relationship has been singled out as crucial in establishing the basic psychodynamics of Jewish humor. It is claimed that the Jewish comic, or schlemiel, remains a "boy-man" even when fully grown, largely because of "the Jewish mother's destructive domination, her demands for love and success from her son which are linked to her refusal to grant him the independence required for manhood."[4] Recent American Jewish literature supplies

4. Albert Goldman, "Boy-man Schlemihl," p. 8.

sufficient testimony on this subject, from the lowbrow *How to be a Jewish Mother* through the black humor of Lenny Bruce and Bruce Jay Friedman, to *Portnoy's Complaint* by Philip Roth. But the example of Herzog would lead us to temper this generalization somewhat, since it suggests that demands for love and success may be constructive as well as the opposite. Most works emphasize the uses of love as a means of domination, and the exaggerated expectations of success as a catalyst to failure. Bellow is one of the very few American Jewish writers to consider and present another interpretation of the same observable phenomena: that love and those expectations explain why Herzog "characteristically, obstinately, defiantly, blindly but without sufficient courage or intelligence tried to be a *marvelous* Herzog, a Herzog who, perhaps clumsily, tried to live out marvelous qualities vaguely comprehended." The family situation, smothering the boy in more love than he would easily find again; endowing him with greater importance than his peers would concede him; placing him at the center of a comprehended circle, whereas he would subsequently find himself floating around some ill-defined circumference; all this blesses the child with a secure sense of self even as it bedevils his later abilities to "get along." Herzog is a "heart's hog,"[5] attempting the marvelous, even as he makes an ironic, schlemiel's progress toward it; and for this his childhood is, as he knows, largely responsible.

Herzog's final self-acceptance has been attacked, and vehemently, as a "fatty sigh of middle-class intellectual contentment."[6] The resolution of the book has been assailed,

5. G. P. Elliot, "Hurtsog, Hairtsog, Heart's Hog?," *Nation*, October 19, 1964, pp. 252–54.
6. John W. Aldridge, "The Complacency of *Herzog*," in *Saul Bellow and the Critics*, ed. Irving Malin (New York, 1967), p. 210.

even by friendly critics, as offering either too little or too
much. Harold Fisch, writing on "The Hero as Jew," con-
curs with the widespread acceptance of *Herzog* as "an attempt to reach beyond mere victim-literature to some more
positive ground of hope" but finds that actually "Herzog
does not *go* anywhere." "The book does not ultimately offer
salvation, and in that sense it fails as a twentieth-century
epistle from the Hebrews."[7] Theodore Solotaroff, by contrast, complains that the conclusion is too affirmative: "The
elegiac prose of the closing section is so naturally luminous
and moving that one tends to overlook the fact that it is
quietly burying most of the issues that earlier had been
raised in connection with its relations to society."[8] And in
fact the general critical tendency has been to find fault with
its ability to resolve at all: "Herzog is finally as arrogantly
complacent in his new-found affirmative position . . . as
Bellow dares to allow him to be."[9]

From the standpoint of schlemiel-literature, this criticism
is entirely beside the point. Insofar as the schlemiel is a
comic hero, he is promised a "happy ending," if not in the
normal sense, then at least in his own self-appraisal. Along
the way we may expect the sacrifice of male initiative, pride,
dignity and socioeconomic achievement—and all of these
expectations are fulfilled—but the conditions of the sacri-
ficial game require that at least one runner, wisely-
chastened, optimistic, self-accepting, must reach base.
When Herzog says (to the horror of critics), "I am pretty
well satisfied to be, to be just as it is willed, and for as long

7. Harold Fisch, "The Hero as Jew: Reflections on *Herzog*," *Judaism*
18, no. 1 (Winter 1968): 52.
8. Theodore Solotaroff, "Napoleon Street and After," *Commentary* 38
(December 1964): 66.
9. Aldridge, "The Complacency of *Herzog*," p. 210.

as I may remain in occupancy," he is within the same convention as virtually all the figures we have previously discussed. In every conceivable empirical test the schlemiel may fail, but he never fails in his final self-acceptance; otherwise the whole premise of the loser-as-victor would be destroyed.

Then, too, criticism of Herzog's complacency does not seem to take into account the degree to which Herzog is an ironic hero, still in the schlemiel tradition. The ironic smugness is present in the very first sentence, for the man who says "If I'm out of my mind, it's all right with me" already appears to be "pretty well satisfied to be just as it is willed." On the other hand, Herzog can go further in self-criticism than even the severest of his critics, and he is usually more unsparing, as well as wittier, in pointing up his own flaws. As he sits, for example, in the city courthouse:

> Herzog discovered that he had been sitting, legs elegantly crossed, the jagged oval rim of his hat pressed on his thigh, his striped jacket still buttoned and strained by his eager posture, that he had been watching all that happened with his look of intelligent composure, of charm and sympathy—like the old song, he thought, the one that goes, "There's flies on me, there's flies on you, but there ain't no flies on Jesus." A man who looked so fine and humane would be outside police jurisdiction, immune to lower forms of suffering and punishment.

Herzog is under no prolonged illusion about his Christlike goodness. He recognizes that his sympathy is socially meaningless and morally fattening, and he mocks it. So too his multifaceted importance to the human race:

> The mirror of the gum machine revealed to Herzog how pale he was, unhealthy—wisps from his coat and wool scarf, his hat and brows, twisting and flaming outward in the overfull light and exposing the sphere of his face, the face of a man who was keeping up a front.

Herzog smiled at this earlier avatar of his life, at Herzog the victim, Herzog the would-be lover, Herzog the man on whom the world depended for certain intellectual work, to change history, to influence the development of civilization. Several boxes of stale paper under his bed in Philadelphia were going to produce this very significant result.

Or again, here is Moses as he sees himself in the frequent role of lover:

And Herzog thought . . . is this really possible? Have all the traditions, passions, renunciations, virtues, gems, and masterpieces of Hebrew discipline and all the rest of it—rhetoric, a lot of it, but containing true facts—brought me to these untidy green sheets, and this rippled mattress?

Surely Solotaroff is right when he says that irony here "takes on the status of an ontological principle." Even the final affirmation follows a crisis of self-doubt: "But this intensity, doesn't it mean anything? Is it an idiot joy that makes this animal, the most peculiar animal of all, exclaim something? And he thinks this reaction a sign, a proof, of eternity?" If Herzog does ultimately accept himself, he does so in the spirit of compromise.

The ending is also typical of schlemiel conclusions in that the character's salvation, not his benevolence, is its exclusive concern. The saint is concerned for others and is canonized for his ability to affect attitudinal or substantive change. While he too, like our hero, risks being thought a fool, his glory is invariably recognized, perhaps posthumously, but without equivocation. Salvation for the schlemiel, to the contrary, is always partial and personal. He does not affirm the objective presence of goodness, but merely the right and the need to believe in it as one component of the human personality. Herzog is always being exposed to social evils, yet always, by his own admission, as a spectator whose concerns are his own feelings and his own conscience. It may be, as Norman Mailer has complained, that with *Herzog* the reality of the novel has coagulated into mere moral earnestness. This is the limitation of all schlemiel works, a seemingly inevitable quality of the genre. What once appeared in the novel as the individual's interaction with his society has now narrowed to a study of the individual's reaction to society. The modern novel of sensibilities does not appear to be a suitable medium for what Mailer calls "cutting a swath across the face of society,"[10] for society is present only insofar as it cuts a swath across the face of the protagonist.

Herzog is, to the dismay of activists, predicated on a certain ineluctable unsatisfactoriness in the environment. Had the novel presented serious possibilities for ameliorative social action, then Herzog's reflective intelligence and his irony would have been a crime. But Herzog is neither judge, counsel, nor defendant. In the critical courtroom sequence he appears as simply one of the millions who must share his place in the city with a woman capable of beating her child to death. If Herzog's pain were the result solely of Madeleine's infidelity and Gersbach's deceit, the "problem of evil" might have seemed chimerical or paranoiac. Had Herzog's knowledge of evil come from his readings, it would have seemed abstract, intellectual. As observer in the courtroom, Herzog becomes a witness to horrors far greater than any in his own experience, and more deeply

10. Norman Mailer, "Modes and Mutations: Quick Comments on the Modern American Novel," *Commentary* 41 (March 1966) : 39. Mailer's own Sam Slovoda, in "The Man Who Studied Yoga," might have been a rather lovable (slob, slovenly) schlemiel had the author not imposed on his character a sour intelligence and the longing to be a hero. As it is, he is "a man who seeks to live in such a way as to avoid pain, and succeeds merely in avoiding pleasure."

personalized than those of history or the daily news. He is exposed to life-size barbarians, his neighbors, in a brutal challenge to his apple-cheeked humanism.

> I fail to understand! thought Herzog, . . . but this is the difficulty with people who spend their lives in humane studies and therefore imagine once cruelty has been described in books it is ended. Of course he really knew better—understood that human beings *would* not live so as to be understood by the Herzogs. Why should they?

Having witnessed the trial, Herzog blindly stumbles away, into the path of a cripple whose "eyes, prominent, severe, still kept him standing, identifying him thoroughly, fully, deeply, as a fool. Again—silently—*Thou fool!*" The events of the sequence remind us of Nathanael West,[11] except that Bellow takes pains to keep Herzog decidedly unsurrealistic. When he is finally alone, Herzog goes over in his mind what he has seen and tries to salvage some human meaning for the murdered boy. It is hardly accidental that the murder dramatized for Herzog is just the sort of murder from which no shred of meaning can be extracted, one which like Auschwitz stands outside the scope of rational thought. Herzog "experienced nothing but his own *human feelings,* in which he found nothing of use." The only resolution he draws—and that irrationally—is to protect his own child.

The courtroom drama is a "play within a play," exploring the subject's relation to what is basest in the modern world. These are horrors that cannot qualify as economic or social problems. Nothing *can* be gained for the murdered boy, no symbolic assurance that the world will be better for his death, no religious murmurings, no personal revelations. Nothing is learned from the murder of this child or from

11. See Leslie Fiedler, *Love and Death in the American Novel* (New York, 1960), p. 464, for a discussion of *Miss Lonelyhearts* as schlemiel-everyman.

the murders of millions of such children. Now Herzog is a kind, thoughtful humanist, and what is he to do with the anguish dumped on his doorstep? His response is not effective, merely affective. When his life touches the uncomfortable, he struggles to understand it. He does not, however, give up his life to it. The irony merely intensifies, as Herzog continues to worry about his soul (*his* soul!) on a trip through Hades. Herzog knows this is petty (petit) and knows also it is necessary because that is his function as a human being. "The strength of a man's virtue or spiritual capacity measured by his ordinary life."

Elsewhere Bellow has written: "We make what we can of our condition with the means available. We must accept the mixture as we find it—the impurity of it, the tragedy of it, the hope of it."[12] It is just this emphasis on *mixture* that distinguishes Herzog and other Jewish schlemiels from the meek Christians like Melville's Billy Budd or Faulkner's fabled corporal. Schlemiels are not creatures of the Manichean imagination: even Charlie Chaplin's *The Great Dictator* divides the alternatives of civilization too sharply between innocence and guilt to be an authentic part of the genre. Though the moral dilemma must always be presented as a confrontation between opposites, its tone is determined by the implied purity of each faction. Herzog and his comic forebears are themselves a little tainted; never having known the primal innocence of Eden, they do not pull up their skirts in outrage at the appearance of villainy, and having no ascetic inclinations, their own chances of "staying clean" are slight. The otherworldly purity of the saints, products of the Christian literary imagination, is best suggested by their silence or stuttering: holiness beyond speech.

12. Saul Bellow, *Great Jewish Short Stories*, p. 16.

The stained humanity of the schlemiel pours out in obsessive verbosity. Yet to say that the polarization between good and evil is less extreme is not to imply that the moral concern is any the less acute. In an article written concurrently with the last parts of *Herzog*, Bellow puts the proposition as follows:

> either we want life to continue or we do not. If we don't want to continue, why write books? The wish for death is powerful and silent. It respects actions; it has no need of words.
>
> But if we answer yes, we do want it to continue, we are liable to be asked how. In what form shall life be justified? That is the essence of the moral question. We call a writer moral to the degree that his imagination indicates to us how we may answer naturally, without strained arguments, with a spontaneous, mysterious proof that has no need to argue with despair.[13]

Herzog is such an attempt at proof.

What sets Herzog apart from the characters previously discussed is his intelligence, and more particularly, his self-consciousness. In *Menahem Mendl*, Sholom Aleichem juxtaposes the life-styles of two characters for ironic effect, but here the protagonist juggles his own distinct levels of existence. Not only does Herzog elucidate his opinions and clarify his feelings, he is able, as an intellectual and a professor of history, to relate those opinions and feelings to the broader flow of Western thought. Thus we find Herzog raising many of his own questions on the nature of the fool:

> he insisted on being the ingénu whose earnestness made his own heart flutter—*zisse n'shamele*, a sweet little soul, Tennie had called Moses. At forty, to earn such a banal reputation! His forehead grew wet. Such stupidity deserved harsher punishment—a sickness, a jail sentence. . . . Still, extreme self-abuse was not really interest-

13. Saul Bellow, "Writer as Moralist," *Atlantic*, March 1963, p. 62.

ing to him, either. . . . Not to be a fool might not be worth the difficult alternatives. Anyway, who was that non-fool? Was it the power-lover, who bent the public to his will . . . the organizational realist? Now wouldn't it be nice to be one? But Herzog worked under different orders—doing, he trusted, the work of the future. The revolutions of the twentieth century, the liberation of the masses by production, created private life but gave nothing to fill it with. This was where such as he came in. The progress of civilization—indeed, the survival of civilization—depended on the successes of Moses E. Herzog.

Is the fool escaping his adult responsibilities, or is he alone fulfilling them? If the only alternatives are the Ayn Rand objectivists and Herzogian innocents, may the progress of civilization not indeed depend upon him?

Not the author or reader, but the character himself raises these questions. Maynard Mack has written that comedy depends on our remaining outside, as spectators, in a position from which we may notice the discrepancies between the facades of personalities as they present themselves, and these personalities as they actually are. "The point of view that ours must be continuous with in comedy is not the character's but the author's."[14] Though true for classical comedy, this description does not fit *Herzog*. Bellow has deliberately—how deliberately only a careful study of syntax will reveal—written the entire book from the character's own point of view, allowing him to observe and note all the discrepancies, and thereby making him the conductor of humor. Because comedy does depend on discrepancies between surface and substance, Herzog is allowed at least two modes of observation: the letters, a direct means of externalizing his concerns; and indirect narration, also re-

14. Maynard Mack, "*Joseph Andrews* and *Pamela*," in *Fielding: A Collection of Critical Essays*, ed. R. Paulson (New Jersey, 1962), p. 58.

flecting the protagonist's point of view, but permitting a wider inclusion of conversation and event. The rapid transition from one to the other sometimes accounts for the comic tone, as when Moses, fleeing from the sex-priestess, Ramona, writes political kudos to Stevenson and Nehru while his unsteady thoughts hurtle him back and forth to and from his personal involvements. More often, within the indirect narration itself, Herzog reveals the self he admires side by side with the self he scorns:

> The house in Ludeyville was bought when Madeleine became pregnant. It seemed the ideal place to work out the problems Herzog had become involved with in *The Phenomenology of Mind* —the importance of the "law of the heart" in Western traditions, the origins of moral sentimentalism and related matters, on which he had distinctly different ideas. He was going—he smiled secretly now, admitting it—to wrap the subject up, to pull the carpet from under all other scholars, show them what was what, stun them, expose their triviality once and for all. It was not simple vanity, but a sense of responsibility that was the underlying motive. That he would say for himself. He was a *bien pensant* type. He took seriously Heinrich Heine's belief that the words of Rousseau had turned into the bloody machine of Robespierre, that Kant and Fichte were deadlier than armies. He had a small foundation grant, and his twenty-thousand-dollar legacy from Father Herzog went into the country place.

The irony of "It seemed" and "He was going" in the second and third sentences derives from the superimposition of Herzog's present knowledge of himself over past hopes. He mocks both his unfulfilled expectations and the very substance of his ideas. The recognition that he is a "bien pensant type" is like his perception, cited earlier, that he is like the old song "There's flies on me, there's flies on you, but there ain't no flies on Jesus." He is ironic about his would-be goodness, suspicious of its motives, and scornful of its inutility. Looking back on the ambitious scholar he was, he smiles at his boy-scout meritoriousness. And the final juxta-position of his sources of income is the unkindest cut of all, the small foundation grant with the big legacy, the earnings of the great intellectual overshadowed by the rewards of the dutiful boy. Here the character, aware and amused by the dismal gap between "is" and "would have been," makes himself his own comic butt.

Herzog's internalization of irony sets him apart from Bloom, from whose saga his name alone is lifted: In *Ulysses*, Joyce has placed in apposition "the persuasive surfaces of personalities as they see themselves, and these characters as they are," even when he seems to be offering a stream of consciousness. The very form of the mock epic imposes the shadow of his heroic predecessor over a dwarfed Bloom. Joyce called his work *Ulysses*, but Herzog casts his own little light. In *Herzog*, the protagonist is en-dowed with the complexity of mind and ironic vision that in *Ulysses* remains the prerogative of the author. The result is not an ironic exposure of life, but rather an ironic life, ex-posed.

Herzog is finally the character who lives according to a twofold perception of himself in relation to the world, both giant and dwarf, alien and center of the universe, failure and success, cuckold and great lover, intellectual and schle-miel. The single reality of the naturalists is for him insuffi-cient. To Sandor Himmelstein, the deformed lawyer, he protests:

"And you think a fact is what's nasty."
"Facts *are* nasty."
"You think they're true because they're nasty."

To James Hoffa, who shares this "angry single-minded-ness," he considers saying: "What makes you think realism must be brutal?" Herzog fights the Wasteland rhetoricians, "The vision of mankind as a lot of cannibals, running in packs, gibbering, bewailing its own murders, pressing out the living world as dead excrement." He points out how corrupting is the effect of this mode of perception on both the individual and on society. Even as he is insisting on the need for the pumping heart, for "moral realities," he jibes at himself:

Do not deceive yourself, dear Moses Elkanah, with childish jingles and Mother Goose. Hearts quaking with cheap and feeble charity or oozing potato love have not written history.

Time and again he makes fun of his search for love and belief in love as a female pursuit, which in the terms of this novel is no flattering tribute. Yet, finally, when all is said and written, Herzog addresses himself seriously, if not earnestly, to his and, as he sees it, the world's situation: "We must get it out of our heads that this is a doomed time, that we are waiting for the end, and the rest of it, mere junk from fashionable magazines." The intellectual rejection of pessimism is ultimately coupled with a psychological readiness to accept, even bless, the future. The ironic life accepts itself. "Anyway, can I pretend that I have much choice?"

Because Herzog's irony is internalized, there is less than the usual ironic distance between author and character. This opens the book to charges of sentimentality, since modern literature and literary criticism are very much concerned with distances and masks, and we are frankly unaccustomed to committing our disbelief to the hands of a reliable narrator. In this work, the author's position or point of view is not noticeably different from the protagonist's. Herzog steers his pumping heart between the Scylla of Madeleine ("Feel? Don't give me that line of platitudes about feelings") and the Charybdis of Valentine, the false commercialized whirlpool of a heart. He controls the novel even when he is not yet in control of himself. Bellow has written a humanist novel, presenting one individual's life—a life by all standards a near-failure—which in its intelligence and energy commands our attention and affection. *Herzog*, a study of irony as a modern form of moral vision, is the more *engagé* because of Saul Bellow's minimal irony about his subject.

7. REQUIEM IN SEVERAL VOICES

Ours is not a hero for all seasons. By the end of the 1960s the Jewish fool began to falter: his ironic balance teetered dangerously between self-indulgence and self-hatred. The writers still drawing on the resources of Jewishness found that the supply lines of the East European culture had been stretched so far in space and time that no rich nourishment remained. To Alexander Portnoy, *Jewish* is a system of repressions with two allowable passions—hatred of the goyim and love of the male child. All the inner stuff of life and ritual, as he perceives it, has been gouged out leaving an empty frame of observance and a feigning of identification or emotion. The traditional culture once insisted that its men got something in return for the sacrifice of their pride and prowess. This claim could have no worth once it appeared that the entire culture had pitiably betrayed itself. A Sunday baseball game played "when the weather is warm enough" does not have the same power to bind and exalt a community as the network of observance that included three daily *minyanim,* assembled in honor of a God who was not known to wait.

Besides, a literature feeds on itself as much as on the living environment. Once the homey and holy uses of Jewish tradition seemed exhausted in modern American writing, writers felt compelled to state the case anew, or to move on to fresh material. One Herzog alone can saturate a theme.

The progress of the schlemiel as a literary hero was more seriously deflected by mounting opposition in the dominant culture, beginning in the mid-1960s, to liberal resignation. Ironic accommodationism, which was intellectually respectable a decade earlier, was denounced as a liberal plot to speed the advent of a fascist state. The Vietnam war, the most persistent war in American history, could not be stopped or contained by those who called it stupid, nor by those who called it tragic, nor even by those who called it genocide. Noam Chomsky and Arthur Schlesinger arguing in the editorial columns of *Commentary* over the meaning of the war seemed, for all their obvious sincerity and information, to be merely an updated version of the Tuneyadevke bathhouse philosophers. As debates lengthened and the war with them, impotence no longer served as proper comic material. The concomitant polarization of left and right in politics and the righteous anger of formerly pacific groups like the blacks and high school students and women, brought on a period of alignment, even a return to ideology. And all activism dismisses the schlemiel. Single-minded—not to say simple-minded—dedication to a particular cause or specific goal cannot tolerate a character whose perception of reality is essentially dualistic. The schlemiel, on his part, is too skeptical of visionary schemes to follow a messianic movement like Marxism and too wary of gloom to accept a fatalistic call like that of the black extremists who declare it is better to die on your feet than live on your knees. One European rabbi is said to have worn a coat with contradictory quotations sewn into the lining of his two pockets. On one side the quotation read: "The world was created for your sake"; on the other, "You are but dust and ashes." Out of the ability to sustain this paradoxical position and to wear such a coat, the irony of East European Jewry grew. But the lifeblood of irony coagulates when a society becomes either wholly optimistic or wholly pessimistic about human potential or God's.

We see the demise of irony reflected in the very literature that gave it such forceful expression. Consciously, or despite their actual intentions, American Jewish writers recreate the familiar character only to prove that he no longer serves.

One sad requiem for the schlemiel is composed by Bernard Malamud, in the six episodes that comprise *Pictures of Fidelman*.[1] In much of his writing, Malamud has been attracted to the weak character for both his comic and tragic qualities. Levin begins *A New Life*[2] when he is pissed on by an aggressive child, and his first lecture is marked by the unusual attention accorded to one who has forgotten to zip up his fly. Yakov Bok, whose surname means goat, is the tragic equivalent of Levin. In *The Fixer*,[3] Malamud has dramatized the most classic case of victimization in recent Jewish history to prove the liberating effects of imprisonment.

Malamud's interest in the Jewish character has not been sociologically determined. Alone among American writers he has fixed on the Jew as representative man—and on the schlemiel as representative Jew. His Jewish Everyman is an isolated, displaced loner, American in Italy, Easterner in the West, German refugee in America, bird among bipeds. Though they sometimes speak with a Yiddish intonation, his heroes bear little actual resemblance to their coreligionists.

1. Bernard Malamud, *Pictures of Fidelman* (New York, 1969).
2. Bernard Malamud, *A New Life* (New York, 1961).
3. Bernard Malamud, *The Fixer* (New York, 1966).

Malamud's failing shopkeepers and starving boarders appear in contemporary fiction as a kind of anachronism; in the works of his contemporaries, like Wallace Markfield, Mordecai Richler, Herbert Gold, such characters are already subjects of nostalgia.

Malamud sees the schlemiel condition as the clearest alternative to the still-dominant religion of success. "The Morris Bobers and S. Levins in Malamud's fictional world succeed as men only by virtue of their failures in society."[4] There is, of course, nothing new about this opposition to success in American fiction. Anti-heroes from the pens of Henry James through James T. Farrell have reached the point of no return by climbing to the doom at the top. But some moderns, Malamud especially, have stated the case positively, for the failures, rather than negatively, against the successes. In Malamud's stories, the protagonist usually has the raw potential for becoming a schlemiel, that is, the potential for suffering, submitting to loss, pain, humiliation, for recognizing himself as, alas, only himself. This potential is sometimes realized, sometimes not. The hero of *A New Life*, S. Levin, wins what the title promises because he takes burdens on himself and follows the bungling path of the loser. A relative, H. Levin, in a story called "The Lady of the Lake,"[5] changes his name and, as he hopes, his status to Freeman, but ends as a slave to his own deception, embracing "only moonlit stone," the symbol of deception. The character courageous enough to accept his ignominy without being crushed by it is the true hero of Malamud's opus, while the man playing the Western hero without admitting to his real identity—Jewish, fearful, suffering, loving, unheroic—is the absolute loser.

4. Sidney Richman, *Bernard Malamud* (New York, 1966), p. 23.
5. Bernard Malamud, "The Lady of the Lake," in *The Magic Barrel* (New York, 1958), pp. 105–33.

Pictures of Fidelman, studies of one more such protagonist, appeared between 1958 and 1969, a span of eleven
years. At the beginning of the series of stories, the main
character is another of Malamud's protests against what he
calls "the colossally deceitful devaluation of man in this
day."[6] By the end, both character and author are dispirited,
possibly because of an overly lengthy association, but more
probably as a result of the growing difficulties in the culture
of keeping such a character alive.

In the first episode, which reads like a Jewish parody of
The Aspern Papers, one Arthur Fidelman, "self-confessed
failure as a painter," turns up in Rome on a carefully
planned and budgeted trip to prepare a study of Giotto.
Fidelman has the good fortune to meet his "Vergil," a moral
guide in the form of Shimon Susskind, who is "a Jewish
refugee from Israel no less." The author's selectivity is nowhere more apparent than in this deliberate distinction between the Jewish type that interests him ("I'm always running") and the Israeli heroism which does not ("the desert
air makes me constipated").

Susskind leads Fidelman to a true understanding of his
own schlemielhood, which is also the process whereby a man

6. Cf. Granville Hicks, "His Hopes on the Human Heart," *Saturday
Review,* October 12, 1963, p. 32: "I am quite tired of the colossally deceitful devaluation of man in this day; for whatever explanation: that
life is cheap amid a prevalence of wars; or because we are drugged by
totalitarian successes into a sneaking belief in their dehumanizing
processes; or tricked beyond self-respect by the values of the creators
of our own thing-ridden society: . . . or because having invented the
means of his extinction, man values himself less for it and lives in daily
dread that he will in a fit of passion, or pique, or absent-mindedness,
achieve his end: Whatever the reason, his fall from grace in his eyes is
betrayed in the words he invented to describe himself as he is now:
fragmented, abbreviated, other-directed, organizational, anonymous
man, a victim, in the words that are used to describe him, of a kind
of synechdochic irony, the part for the whole. The devaluation exists
because he accepts it without protest."

becomes a *mentsh,* as Hassan has so quotably put it. The unredeemed Fidelman's crime is his refusal to part with his suit. As he justifiably explains to the schnorrer, Susskind, "All I have is a change from the one you now see me wearing." Though Fidelman's crime is mere parsimony, and though he does give up five banknotes in his eagerness to rid himself of Susskind, the acts of withholding and of giving only under duress, confirm that Fidelman is unsatisfactory in human responses. He is too measured, both in taking and giving. He is even afraid of his passion for history: "This kind of excitement was all right up to a point, perfect maybe for a creative artist, but less so for a critic. A critic, he thought, should live on beans." Susskind takes it upon himself to be the visiting American's "guide."

Cruel to be kind, Susskind steals the budding scholar's opening chapter on Giotto, and as we later learn, consigns it to the flames. The disorientation Fidelman experiences after the loss of his chapter is the first hopeful sign of his development; his quest for the manuscript, orderly at first, then increasingly frantic, is accompanied by the disintegration of his former self. He cannot go on with the meticulous note-taking; he rearranges his studied schedule of travel, this time improvising; he frequents movie houses instead of museums, sees the prostitutes in the street, not merely those on canvas; and, eventually, tracking Susskind down, he is exposed to misery in a form and degree unknown to him before. Slowly, he learns.

The redemption is not complete until after a visit to Susskind's room, a visit from which "he never fully recovered." Fidelman brings Susskind the suit he has so consistently denied him. But Fidelman has yet to grasp the full interconnection between life and art. In return for his suit, Susskind returns the empty briefcase, revealing that ·its content, the Giotto chapter, has been destroyed.

"I did you a favor," says Susskind, "The words were there but the spirit was missing."

Vergilio Susskind thus leads Fidelman into the final humiliating perception of the failure of all he had previously aspired to as success. The acceptance of failure is the crucial moment of initiation, as when Yakov Bok accepts his imprisonment, or when Frankie Alpine accepts himself as Jew. Now, reconciled to failure, Fidelman can proceed to live out his comic humanity.

This first episode, called "The Last Mohican," tells a fairly standard story, and we are all antipriggish enough to appreciate a bit of *Pull Down Vanity*.[7] A repressed American critic in oxblood shoes with a neat schedule of inquiry is itching to be reformed, and nothing in the denouement is surprising or displeasing. But when Fidelman next turns up as an inferior painter, paying, like Gimpel the Fool, far more than he should for the privilege of loving an Italian *pittrice*, the theme of failure intensifies. Malamud challenges the last remnant of the hero-myth in Western culture, the myth of the artist as the final embodiment of that noble quest for purity and truth. Fidelman is not fearlessly independent but the enslaved toilet cleaner and copyist for a pair of small-time art thieves. Fidelman is not perfect in his moral radiance but a cheap procurer, and a not-too-successful one at that. Above all, Fidelman is a bad artist, as inferior a craftsman as the Bratslaver's simple man was a bad shoemaker. No matter how intimate his knowledge of life or how edifying his many adventures of body and soul, his art never improves. He works among compromises, with dictated subjects, tools, circumstances. This is a generalized portrait of the artist as schlemiel, a man

7. Leslie Fiedler, *Pull Down Vanity* (Philadelphia, 1962). The title story pulls down the vanity of a professor of creative writing.

drawn on the same scale as other men, small and silly, but involved in a recognizably human enterprise.

The adventures of Fidelman become increasingly zany, keeping pace with the subject's experiments in painting and the author's growing ambivalence about his character. By the penultimate episode, from which the book's title is taken, the frenetic, staccato pace gives the uncomfortable impression that Fidelman's time has run out, like a wound-up doll that is stumbling to a halt after a lengthy dance. The "pictures" are hurried impressions of the subject in real and imagined poses. While Fidelman does not seem appreciably different, the cost of his style of living has risen so sharply that the gentle ironies have worn thin, revealing much harsher ones: "Fidelman pissing in muddy waters discovers water over his head." Language, imagery, and the hero, have lost the innocence of earlier episodes. The quick impression of church art, as summarized by Fidelman, is a house of horrors:

Lives of the Saints. S. Sebastian, arrow collector, swimming in bloody sewer. Pictured transfixed with arrows. S. Denis, decapitated. Pictured holding his head. S. Agatha, breasts shorn clean running enflamed. Painted carrying both bloody breasts in white salver. S. Stephen crowned with rocks. Shown stoned. S. Lucy tearing out eyes for suitor smitten by same. Portrayed bearing two-eyed omelet on dish . . .

The artist's vision runs amok. Withdrawing completely from representational art, and from human life, Fidelman tries digging perfect holes, travelling from place to place with his mobile exhibition. The holes are graves, the death of expression. Fidelman's soul is in obvious danger, and as in the opening story, Susskind appears as savior. There, events were plotted realistically, and if certain images rose to the level of symbols, they were still embedded in the actual events of the story. But by this point the lines between realism and symbolism have disappeared, as in the mind of one who can no longer accurately distinguish between fact and fancy. Susskind is Sussking, the reincarnated Christ, preaching the new gospel. "Tell the truth. Don't cheat. If its easy it don't mean its good. Be kind, specially to those that they got less than you." Fidelman in this frame is the guilt-ridden Judas who sells his redeemer for thirty-nine pieces of silver and "runneth out to buy paints, brushes, canvas." The morality of the artist is the betrayal of goodness. The final "picture" has Fidelman as "the painter in the cave," an artistic Plato, trying to capture pure ideas in pure geometric designs. Susskind reappears in the cave of shadows as the source of light—a one-hundred-watt light bulb. The bulb is the Hebraic light giving out its moral message to the Hellenized painter, telling him to go upstairs to "say hello to your poor sister who hasn't seen you in years." Bessie, his source of support over the years, is dying, and it would make her so happy to see her brother Arthur again. At first Fidelman insists on staying put and painting out his perfect truths on the walls of the cave, but eventually he gives up his "graven images" long enough to fulfill his obligation, to go upstairs and say his last goodbye. "Bessie died and rose to heaven, holding in her heart her brother's hello." The standard bedside leave-taking, although here in a parodistic form, does not entirely cancel out the underlying seriousness of Fidelman's decision. The closing line is "natura, morta. Still life," echo of a previous motif, the counterpoint of dead nature, yet still, life.

Because he is a human animal, the artist dare not deal in Platonic purities; there is someone dying in the room upstairs to whom he is accountable and whose imperfections he shares. To live within the comedy of human limitation, while striving to create the aesthetic verities in some eternal form—that is the artistic equivalent to the schlemiel's suspension between despair and hope. Between the house of horrors that opens the story—art like Francis Bacon's that lingers over the brutal and the grotesque—and the escape from reality, represented by the empty holes and geometric forms to which Fidelman turns for solace, lies the real task of art, the confrontation with Bessie. From her Fidelman first escaped to Rome, and it is to her, to the "too complicated" (repeated three times) past that she represents that he returns. But the prolonged unwillingness of Fidelman to leave his purities, and the tortured difficulties of the style, point strongly to the increasing difficulty of maintaining schlemiel irony. In fact, the concluding episode called "Glass Blower of Venice," is a labored story, dragging its sad weight along much as its hero drags his customers piggyback across the flooded piazza.

Fidelman enters his final metamorphosis, as craftsman and bisexual lover. Not finding everything he seeks in the mythical Margherita, he is taken over by her husband, Beppo. "Fidelman had never in his life said 'I love you' without reservation to anyone. He said it to Beppo. If that's the way it works, that's the way it works. Better love than no love. If you sneeze at life it backs off and instead of fruits you're holding a bone." A homosexual with hemorrhoids is the contemporary candidate for the role of victimized male, seeing that representations of the cuckold and rejected suitor are outworn. By taking upon himself the burden of this unsanctioned love, Fidelman becomes a still more faithful human adventurer, for only the man with the heaviest load is, according to Malamud's perception, the realized being.

What distinguishes this story from earlier ones is its

utterly cheerless tone, and its fatal self-consciousness. As
if holding the bone were insufficient, Fidelman learns to love
his man as he learns to blow glass. The two are one, and the
paragraph describing this double education ends with the
prescription: "If you knew how, you could blow anything,"
the author blowing up his own metaphor with a rude bray.
Beppo slashes up all Fidelman's canvases on the theory that
no art is better than bad art, and by accepting this harsh
judgment the painter is supposed to prove his mastery over
a bad fate. Beppo, like Susskind, teaches the gospel of failure as the beginning of wisdom.

Fidelman, now the wiser adventurer, returns home where,
we are told, "he worked as a craftsman in glass and loved
men and women." Yet this time the internal evidence of the
story is unconvincing, and it contains nothing to warrant our
faith in the upbeat conclusion. The life of Fidelman has
grown as heavy as the punning. Humor has descended to
scatology, from heart to rectum. The author repeats a process he has already described, but without conviction. Final
pictures of Fidelman are of a comic strip caricature, a poor
stumblebum whose failures remain unmitigated. The price
of failure hardly seems worth the prize.

A second unredeemed schlemiel is Alexander Portnoy,[8]
the most popular protagonist of American fiction since
George F. Babbitt. Portnoy, as he readily admits, is the
character in the Jewish joke, the straight man, the Jewish
mother's Lemuel Pitkin. And as both author and character
agree, the boy is sick: Portnoy accepts the psychoanalytic
verdict that the loser is a masochist, and taking sexual liberation as the key to total freedom he tries to venture beyond
irony to Norman O. Brown's magic country of love not
death.

---

8. Philip Roth, *Portnoy's Complaint* (New York, 1969).

Unlike the ancestors from whom he inherits all too much, Portnoy is unwilling to suffer limitation or postponement of desire since he is not convinced that the sacrifice is necessary. More American than Jew, he wants his peaches floating in jello, and he wants to eat them too. In his family's mouth all references to Jewish calamities are overworked clichés, and Portnoy sees no reason to rehearse the old set of responses once the objective causes for self-repression seem no longer to exist. The price of Jewish containment is, clearly, piles. Though he has heard *and* heard the litany of Jewish persecutions, he himself stands in the bright ahistoric present. When Alexander is invited to Elm Street, and American pumpkins fall at his feet, inherited reflexes of a pogrom-threatened enclave are inappropriate and self-defeating.

To his real malady, and most significant inheritance, Portnoy makes no reference: he is a verbalizer whose essential experience is linguistic. The real masturbation of the book is verbal, the orgasms are literary climaxes. Roth's approach to sex is pure antipornography; the sharp cross-cutting between different time zones and levels of fantasy takes the very intellectual form of wit. The hero aspires to sensual pleasure, but the true sensuality is the manipulation of grammar. The character's technique of "avoidance and sublimation" is the creation of those same Jewish jokes from whose grip he seeks to free himself. The form of the book is, after all, a joke, a very timely, very funny joke. Its method is not psychoanalysis at all, but satire.

Portnoy's energetic endeavor to achieve a guilt-free pleasurable life culminates in Israel, the same land that appeared briefly in Uris's *Exodus*, healthy preserve of the six-foot sabra. Here poor Portnoy is unmanned and unmasked as "ironical," "self-depreciating," character of "ghetto humor," and climactically, "schlemihl!" Sex may not have been altogether satisfactory before, but at least he has had it. In this all-female country where every tractor driver is his mother and the men are so mythologically potent they are forever "up in the mountains," Portnoy falls impotent. He becomes at the last a whimpering victim, ending his shame in the classic American gangster finale, the guilt-ridden masturbator transformed into the bullet-ridden criminal.

Despite the resemblance of this extended monologue to earlier schlemiel writings, it is a reaction to, not an addition to, the genre. The author defines his hero's complaint as "a disorder in which strongly-felt ethical and altruistic impulses are perpetually warring with extreme sexual longings, often of a perverse nature." The book does not mediate but exacerbates the conflict between these warring claims without ever suggesting that their mutual coexistence may be the cheapest price to be paid for "civilization." Portnoy's complaint presents the schlemiel condition as unbearable; and for all its dialect-humor the punch line seriously implies that the purgation of the narrative ought to be the starting point in the cure. The Jewish joke was conceived as an instrument for turning pain into laughter. *Portnoy's Complaint* reverses the process to expose the full measure of pain lurking beneath the laughter, suggesting that the technique of adjustment may be worse than the situation it was intended to alleviate.

We are back in a new enlightenment, and as the group is thought to have control over its destiny, it must be satirized for failing to execute its proper task. There is no toleration for irony, although irony is the hero's life-style, not to mention the author's, and the willingness to retire with the philosophic shrug, "Oy, civilization and its discontents," is considered a betrayal of joyous potential. The self-hatred of which most unfavorable critics accuse the book grows from the rather self-loving notion that we could be better if only we tried, the tired but persistent thesis of the little engine that could. By this light, the little man who couldn't ceases to be the model of humanity and becomes again the mockery of its failings.

Alongside the fictional autobiography of Philip Roth appeared the factual autobiography of his contemporary, Norman Podhoretz, who similarly passes over his life for clues to the riddle of how he got this way. Podhoretz focuses on the social aspects of the question for which his sober confession is a perfect vehicle. The book opens in aggressive immediacy:

> Let me introduce myself: I am a man who at the precocious age of thirty-five experienced an astonishing revelation: it is better to be a success than a failure.[9]

With unhurried intelligence, Podhoretz discusses the public parts of his life, stopping to analyze the relations between his experience and the social principles guiding it. The author unfolds a typical tale of the bright second-generation Jewish son who rises to eminence in his chosen profession, but his account is atypical in its unambiguous conclusion. Success stories of ambitious young men are expected to turn on the inner failure that poisons the fruits of their achievement. The model for such works in American Jewish writing is Abraham Cahan's *The Rise of David Levinsky* in which the hero's emotional sterility is the predictable price for his financial satiety; the same theme virtually dominates modern fiction in Europe and America. Podhoretz's admirable challenge to this accepted notion redefines "making it" as exactly that, the fulfillment of a man's ambitions and the

9. Norman Podhoretz, *Making It* (New York, 1967), p. ix.

wholesome ability to recognize and savor his exploits.

Only by a determined avoidance of personal disclosures is the author able to keep his findings irony-free, for what few hints we are thrown on the subject of family and friends suggest that a total biography might have been considerably more equivocal than this professional one. Yet, oddly enough, in an atmosphere of chest-baring egotism, the firm avoidance of intimate information becomes one of the book's most endearing qualities, and a hope of the author's maturity in even that domain.

Making It is the unmaking of a schlemiel. The boy's natural will to succeed comes into conflict with the "cult of failure" which in its crudest form decries the pushiness of an aggressive Jew, and at its most refined, questions the ethical propriety of all aggression. Caught and for many years confused by these mixed messages, the author pulls apart the entangled strands of his education and proposes that the WASP lessons in gentility are a fraud. Several years back, Seymour Krim, in *Shots of a Near-Sighted Cannoneer*, wrote about unmaking it, where he questioned the fraudulent emphasis on achievement as defined by New York intellectuals, but that was another movie and, in fact, a lesser one.

The "family" into which Podhoretz is accepted and the kingdom he comes to rule may easily be dismissed as lilliputian, yet the tendency to measure all achievement by mythical standards of greatness is just another way of belittling or avoiding the recognition of any achievement whatever, another legacy of the failure cult.

Philip Roth passionately pleads against the schlemiel inheritance for its crippling effect on the psyche. Podhoretz calmly, though with no less passion, sets himself against the schlemiel inheritance for its crippling effect on the polity.

The "alienated" ghettoized Jew or intellectual never feels "anything but completely powerless in relation to what might or might not go on 'out there,' " and feeling powerless, he is comfortably irresponsible. The man who asserts without apology that his experience, "however unrepresentative or peripheral or exotic it might seem, was a valid sample of life in America which could be used to illuminate even the most centrally significant of American problems," that man is taking an immense risk of involvement, but the courage to do it constitutes political manhood.

For Podhoretz the ironic acceptance of failure, particularly within the American context, is not merely a personal tragedy, as it is for Roth, but a monstrous sociopolitical mistake that works against the abdicating group and more lethally to the detriment of democratic society. His bildungsroman, like all works in that genre, the description of an education intended to provide an education, reveals that failure is also a bitch-goddess, with a special attraction for the sensitive and the educated, and with far less savory personal and social rewards than that of her classy sister.

Whether for reasons of gloom, exotic self-indulgence, opulent self-hatred, or a new dedication to reform, the schlemiel is being rejected as a hero in contemporary American writing. No one, I think, could argue that balanced irony is the perfect human response to life's miseries. The strength of civilization depends on our skills in diagnosing and ameliorating its present evils, tasks which require a vigorous, wholehearted engagement. So the declining fortunes of the schlemiel may be interpreted—by those of us who persist in reading literature as a form of prophesy—to mean that faith in the ability to improve our world is now strong enough to vanquish skepticism. On the other hand, and there is usually another hand, it may also be that skepticism about the ability to improve the world is so strong as to have killed all hope.

Whatever his immediate future, the natural buoyancy of the schlemiel certainly encourages our belief in his long-range survival. Like the dybbuk of Ghenghis Cohn, he will probably be around to haunt someone.

APPENDIX

The most detailed etymological inquiry into the term *schlemiel* (*schlemihl, shlemiel,* etc.) can be found in Dov Sadan's Hebrew article, "Lesugia:shlumiel" [On the problem of the schlemiel] in *Orlogin* 1 (December 1950) : 198–203. Professor Sadan establishes the currency of the word in German usage before the nineteenth century, citing in particular Grimm's dictionary in which the word is traced to Jewish underworld slang, and to the Hebrew word *schlimazl,* meaning luckless. Bringing numerous examples from Hebrew and Yiddish writing, Professor Sadan shows that the term generally refers to the good and devoted man who has no luck, who is either accidentally or characteristically a prey to misfortune.

But Professor Sadan attributes the widespread popularity of the term directly to Chamisso's novel *Peter Schlemihl,* which decisively turned the proper name of its protagonist into a common noun. The essay asks why Chamisso should have selected this particular term and whether there was any conscious recourse to a Jewish name. Although Professor Sadan cannot substantiate the claim that Chamisso thought of his protagonist as a Jew, he analyzes the book to show that Peter Schlemihl is subconsciously modelled on the figure of Ahasuerus, the Wandering Jew, and that the lack of a shadow (which all other men possess) is the closest metaphorical equivalent for the lack of a homeland (which all other men possess). He also shows that in the works of many of Chamisso's German-Jewish contemporaries, the term *schlemiel* came to be used in a fairly specific way: not for the simple bungler, but to represent the man fated to be different, homeless, alien, and Jewish.

Of course Professor Sadan also refers to the most famous etymological explanation for the term, Heinrich Heine's bogus claim, in *Hebrew Melodies*, that the name originates with Herr Schlemihl ben Zurishaddai, head of the tribe of Simeon (Numbers 7:36), who was killed accidentally by the irate Phineas as he was trying to assassinate Zimri, thereby introducing for all time the type of the hapless victim. Heine called all poets the descendants of that first schlemiel. Professor Sadan says wryly that the creator of the prototypical schlemiel was himself its embodiment— Heine's statue, like Peter Schlemihl's shadow, being banished from his native soil and finally finding refuge only in the unlikely harbor of New York.

BIBLIOGRAPHY

This bibliography includes works which are discussed in the body of the text, or which have been particularly helpful in the formation of its ideas.

Arendt, Hannah. "The Jew as Pariah." In *Arguments and Doctrines: A Reader of Jewish Thinking in the Aftermath of the Holocaust*, pp. 24–49. Ed. Arthur A. Cohen. New York, 1970.

Ausubel, Nathan, ed. *A Treasury of Jewish Humor*. New York, 1951.

Bal Makhshoves (Eliashev). "Sholom Aleichem." In *Geklibene shriftn*, 1:91–103. Vilna, 1910.

Bellow, Saul. *Dangling Man*. New York, 1944.

———. *Herzog*. New York, 1964.

———, ed. *Great Jewish Short Stories*. New York, 1963.

Bergson, Henri. "Laughter." In *Comedy*, pp. 61–190. Ed. Wylie Sypher. New York, 1956.

Bernshteyn, Ignats. *Yidishe shprikhverter un redensarten* [Yiddish proverbs]. Warsaw, 1908.

Bialostotski, B. J. *Yidisher humor un yidishe letsim* [Jewish humor and Jewish fools]. New York, 1963.

Blair, Walter. *Horse Sense in American Humor*. Chicago, 1942.

Borowski, Tadeusz. *This Way for the Gas, Ladies and Gentlemen*. New York, 1968.

Buber, Martin. *The Tales of Rabbi Nachman*. Trans. Maurice Friedman, Bloomington, Ind., 1962.

Chamisso, Adalbert von. *Peter Schlemihl*. Trans. Leopold von Lowenstein-Wertheim. In *Three Great Classics*. New York, 1964.

Charles, Gerda, ed. *Modern Jewish Stories*. London and Englewood Cliffs, N. J., 1963.

Eastman, Max. *The Sense of Humor*. New York, 1921.

Erik, Max. *Di geshikhte fun der yidisher literatur fun di eltste tsaytn biz der Haskole tkufe* [History of Yiddish Literature from its beginnings till the Haskalah]. Warsaw, 1928.

Fiedler, Leslie. *The Jew in the American Novel*. New York, 1959.

————. *Love and Death in the American Novel*. New York, 1960.

————. *Waiting for the End*. New York, 1964.

Friedman, Bruce Jay. *Stern*. New York, 1962.

————. *A Mother's Kisses*. New York, 1964.

Freud, Sigmund. *Jokes and Their Relation to the Unconscious*. Trans. James Strachey. New York, 1960.

Goldman, Albert. "Boy-man, Schlemihl: The Jewish Element in American Humor." In *Explorations*, pp. 3–17. Ed. Murray Mindlin and Chaim Bermant. London, 1967.

Hemingway, Ernest. *The Sun Also Rises*. New York, 1926.

Howe, Irving. *A World More Attractive: A View of Modern Literature and Politics*. New York, 1963.

————, and Greenberg, Eliezer, eds. *A Treasury of Yiddish Stories*. New York, 1953.

Kahan, Y[ehuda] L[eib], ed. *Yidisher folklor*. Vilna, 1938.

Knox, Israel. "The Traditional Roots of Jewish Humor." In *Judaism* 12, no. 3 (Summer 1963) : 327–37.

Koestler, Arthur. *Arrival and Departure*. London, 1943.

Landmann, Salcia. *Jüdische Witze*. Munich, 1962.

————. *Jüdische Anekdoten und Sprichwörter*. Munich, 1965.

Mailer, Norman. "Modes and Mutations: Quick Comments on the Modern American Novel." In *Commentary* 41, no. 3 (March 1966) : 37–40.

Malamud, Bernard. *The Assistant*. New York, 1957.

————. *The Magic Barrel*. New York, 1958.

————. *A New Life*. New York, 1961.

————. *Idiots First*. New York, 1963.

————. *The Fixer*. New York, 1966.

————. *Pictures of Fidelman*. New York, 1969.

Malin, Irving. ed. *Saul Bellow and the Critics*. New York, 1967.

Manger, Itsik. *Megile lider*. Warsaw, 1936.

Markfield, Wallace. *To an Early Grave*. New York, 1964.

Mendele Mocher Sforim (Abramovitch). *Ale verk*. Vilna, Warsaw, and New York, 1911–13.

————. *Fishke the Lame*. Trans. Gerald Stillman. New York, 1960.

————. *The Nag*. Trans. Moshe Spiegel. New York, 1955.

————. *The Travels and Adventures of Benjamin III*. Trans. Moshe Spiegel. New York, 1949.

Nahman ben Simhah. *Seyfer sipurey masyot* [Stories]. New York, 1951.

Niger, Shmuel. *Vegn yidishe shrayber*. Warsaw, 1912.

———— and I. Shatski, eds. *Leksikon fun der nayer yidisher literatur*. New York, 1956–68.

Oislender, N. *Gruntshtrikhn fun yidishn realism* [Basic characteristics of Yiddish realism]. Vilna, 1928.

————. "Der yunger Sholom Aleichem un zayn roman, *Stempenyu*." In *Shriftn fun der Katedre far Yidisher Kultur bay der Alukraynisher Visnshaftlekher Akademie*, Kiev, 1 (1928): 5–72.

Olsvanger, Immanuel, ed. *Royte pomerantsen*. New York, 1947.

Paley, Grace. *The Little Disturbances of Man*. New York, 1959.

Pearson, Gabriel. "Bellow, Malamud, and Jewish Arrival." In *Explorations*. Ed. M. Mindlin and C. Bermant. London, 1967.

Podhoretz, Norman. *Making It*. New York, 1967.

Ravnitski, J. Kh. *Yidishe vitsn*. 2 vols. New York, 1950.

Reik, Theodor. *Jewish Wit*. New York, 1962.

Richman, Sidney. *Bernard Malamud*. New York, 1966.

Rosenfeld, Isaac. *An Age of Enormity: Life and Writing in the Forties and Fifties*. Cleveland and New York, 1962.

Rosten, Leo Calvin (Leonard Q. Ross). *The Education of H*Y*M*A*N K*A*P*L*A*N*. New York, 1937.

Roth, Philip. *Goodbye, Columbus*. Boston, 1959.

————. *Portnoy's Complaint*. New York, 1969.

Rourke, Constance. *American Humor: A Study of the National Character*. New York, 1931.

Samuel, Maurice. *The World of Sholom Aleichem*. New York, 1943.

————. *The Gentleman and the Jew.* New York, 1950.

Sholom Aleichem (Rabinovitch). *Ale verk.* 28 vols. New York, 1937.

————. *Adventures of Mottel, the Cantor's Son.* Trans. Tamara Kahana. New York, 1953.

————. *Selected Stories.* Ed. Alfred Kazin. New York, 1956.

————. *Tevye's Daughters.* Trans. Frances Butwin. New York, 1949.

————. *The Adventures of Menahem Mendl.* Trans. Tamara Kahana. New York, 1969.

Schwartz-Bart, André. *Le dernier des justes.* Paris, 1959.

Singer, Isaac Bashevis. *Gimpel the Fool and Other Stories.* New York, 1957.

————. *Gimpl Tam un andere dertseylungen.* New York, 1963.

————. *Short Friday and Other Stories.* New York, 1964.

————. *The Spinoza of Market Street.* New York, 1961.

Solotaroff, T. "Napoleon Street and After." *Commentary* 38 (December 1964) : 63–66.

Stutchkof, Nahum. *Der oytser fun der yidisher shprakh* [Yiddish thesaurus]. New York, 1950.

Tanner, Tony. *Saul Bellow.* Edinburgh and London, 1965.

Thompson, J. A. K. *Irony, A Historical Introduction.* London, 1926.

Trunk, I. I. *Tevye un Menakhem Mendl in yidishn velt goyrl* [Tevye and Menahem Mendl as expressions of Jewish fate]. New York, 1944.

Viner, M. *Tsu der geshikhte fun der yidisher literatur in 19tn yorhundert.* New York, 1945.

————. *Vegn Sholom Aleykhem's Humor.* Moscow, 1941.

Welsford, Enid. *The Fool, His Social and Literary History.* Gloucester, Mass., 1966.

West, Nathanael. *The Complete Works of Nathanael West.* New York, 1957.

INDEX